Kohn Pedersen Fox
Architecture and Urbanism
2003–2012

*First published in the United States of America
by Rizzoli International Publications, Inc.
300 Park Avenue South, New York, NY 10010
www.rizzoliusa.com*

*Kohn Pedersen Fox: Architecture and Urbanism 2003–2012
Copyright © 2012 Kohn Pedersen Fox Associates, with text
contributions by John Bushell, Joshua Chaiken, Peter
Murray, Paul Katz, James von Klemperer, A. Eugene Kohn,
Jill N. Lerner, William C. Louie, Anthony Mosellie,
William Pedersen.*

*For Kohn Pedersen Fox Associates
Editors: Anita Franchetti & David Niles
Editorial Oversight: James von Klemperer
Image Coordinator: John Chu*

*For Rizzoli International Publications
Editors: Ian Luna & Lauren A. Gould
Managing Editor: Ellen Nidy
Editorial Coordinator: Mandy DeLucia
Editorial Assistant: Kayleigh Jankowski
Production: Kaija Markoe
Book Design: Eugene Lee*

*Printed in Hong Kong SAR
2011 2012 2013 2014 2015 / 10 9 8 7 6 5 4 3 2 1
Library of Congress Control Number: 2012939537
ISBN: 978-0-8478-3860-8*

Foreword

This book represents ten years of the work of Kohn Pedersen
Fox completed between 2002 and 2012, and is the fourth in
the Rizzoli series on the firm. Unlike previous volumes, only
built projects are shown. The intention is to focus on the
craft of architecture, the manifestation of design in specific
material solutions. The only exception to this rule is the
last chapter on city planning efforts, where completion of
work is marked by the beginning rather than the end of a
construction process.

Projects are ordered not chronologically, but by use (typology)
and by form (morphology). This allows the reader to compare
like projects, and understand how similar challenges
are handled in a variety of ways, across a wide range of
contextual circumstances. This grouping displays the balance
between continuity and variety of architectural approaches
in the firm's work.

Over the past decade KPF has grown in size from 300
to 600 staff, maintaining its central hub in New York,
complemented by a substantial presence in London. New
offices were established in Shanghai, Hong Kong, Seoul, and
Abu Dhabi, serving as local centers for project supervision and
communication. Despite this increase in numbers, KPF has
maintained the spirit of a smaller practice where the creation
of design and the production of buildings revolve around a
close conversation within a cohesive community of architects.

Table of Contents

In Conversation:
A. Eugene Kohn & William Pedersen

With Peter Murray

1

Sunday July 4 1976, the 200th Anniversary of the signing of the Declaration of Independence and the culmination of the celebrations marking the Bicentenary, was an auspicious day.

As the great American Birthday Party got under way and a fleet of tall ships sailed up the Hudson River, three architects met for lunch at the Rye Hilton in Westchester to outline the goals for the firm they were about to start. A. Eugene Kohn, William Pedersen and Shelly Fox signed their own declaration of intent and shook hands. Despite the fact that they were launching the practice in the depths of a major recession the three were confident they could make it work.

The roots of the association went back to the days when Shelly Fox and Gene Kohn studied together at the University of Pennsylvania. Upon graduation, they both went off to the Korean War. Shelly to the Army, Gene to the Navy where he served on active duty for three years before taking up a place at graduate school at Penn where he studied under Louis Kahn, Romaldo Giurgola and Robert Venturi.

In 1967 Kohn joined the recently opened New York office of the California-based architect John Carl Warnecke. Warnecke had been a favored architect of the Kennedy administration and selected by Mrs. Kennedy to design the tomb of the assassinated President. Kohn brought Fox into the firm in 1972.

"At that point I wasn't thinking of starting my own firm," says Kohn. "I felt I was lucky to have a job. I had the responsibility initially of running the New York office, and then the whole firm when I became its President. I was really interested in

building up Warnecke as a great design group. I had heard about Bill Pedersen while Bill was working on the East Wing of the National Gallery in Washington with I. M. Pei. I remember someone telling me that Bill would become one of the great designers, period, and what a nice human being he was, so I made up my mind to pursue him."

"Jim Nash, who I worked with at Pei's office, had gone to Warnecke's office and suggested that I meet with Gene," Bill continues. "The first time he suggested the idea, we were in the middle of the National Gallery project, but a year later, that was pretty well under control; I could see there weren't the opportunities in Pei's organization for me to be able to achieve what I hoped to achieve in architecture, but when I interviewed with Gene I could see that here was an opportunity to design more independently."

Pedersen joined Warnecke as the head designer in the firm but it was not an easy time. The recession of 1973 had a major impact on workloads and there was a staggering 60% unemployment among architects.

"Warnecke at that time began to make cuts to his staff without giving a lot of thought to the future and the return to a better economy."says Gene. "I realized I didn't have a long-term future working in that climate. I had built up a good relationship with Bill and Shelly and we were good friends. Shelly and I were very different. Shelly was like my father. Very conservative, very strict, precise, disciplined, always on time, always looked like he just got out of the shower. He never looked tired. He was a marvelously organized guy. A decent

2

3

4

5

human being and a very good manager. And it occurred to me that the three of us would make a very good team."

They had a go at proposing a deal with Warnecke where they stayed on as partners, but that didn't work out.

"Warnecke turned us down" Kohn continues "and that led to us thinking about moving on. But the problem was the state of the economy. There seemed to be no work. Bill was thinking of going back to Minnesota and doing some houses there. My parents thought I was crazy wanting to leave Warnecke's. We all had families and it was a big move. But with Bill's talent and Shelly's abilities I knew we could do it."

It is the dynamic of that partnership that has powered the practice of KPF to its leading role in contemporary architecture. Kohn became the new firm's president and partner in charge of projects; Pedersen was the designer; and Fox oversaw administration and finance. Bill Pedersen uses the analogy of the sail boat to describe the synergy between the triumvirate.

"There are the three constituent parts, you have a keel, you have a hull and you have the sails. I've always felt that Shelly Fox undoubtedly took the role of the keel, Gene is the sail—he was the driving force. That relationship of the individuals, and the way we work together in respect of each other's roles, each other's boundaries is very much related to the way we design, and the way we design is based on the specific condition we find ourselves in.

"The way we work closely with clients comes out of our personalities. That's the way we are. When our clients have issues which are of great concern to them, we find a way of solving them. This is the DNA of the firm. Our role is that of essentially commercial architects. I don't use that in any pejorative sense. Our opportunities came to us early on through Gene's relationships and connections, and those led us to design those buildings that are largely the buildings that cities are built with: the commercial office building. It is a humble type, but it is the building type that makes the backdrop of the modern city, and we made it our aim to help these buildings contribute to the city in ways they hadn't contributed before. That is the beginning of it all; it hasn't really changed over all the years."

The period prior to the founding of the firm, the 1960s and 1970s had produced some of the worst building for cities.

"I remember when we had that first lunch," Gene adds, "we talked about what our goals would be. We chose to pursue commercial architecture because we felt that what was happening to our cities was pretty terrible on account of these buildings. Since they influence our daily lives so much, it was important to do something great with them, really make them work. So that became our goal and our mission."

The chemistry between the trio worked. Clients used to comment to Gene how good it was to work with them because they seemed to enjoy and respect each other; they had fun together, but also did great things together. Each of the partners wanted to stay active as architects, while handling other aspects of the firm, whether it was marketing, staffing, or contracts.

"One of our key aims was to build the firm to last longer and beyond our active days," says Gene. "So we wanted to bring in young people, working with them, motivating them and teaching them so that hopefully one day they would become partners and take over. That was the goal. We always felt that we wanted to bring on people who were as good or better than ourselves to be the future leaders, as opposed to people we were better than, because you can't have a great firm unless you have talent that replaces you."

"I think that comes out of the basic nature of the personalities that are involved," adds Bill. "Gene is an enormously supportive person. He is always encouraging, he is always building other people up, he's making them feel good about themselves, primarily because he feels good about himself! And that role of being supportive of people has been totally responsible for the growth and dynamic of the firm, because the young people that are leading the firm now are terrific individuals, they have abilities that in many cases exceed our abilities, and we freely acknowledge that."

The three partners' skills were totally complementary. "Shelly had great management skills, bookkeeping," says Gene. "He was very organized. Bill is a great designer, no question. And myself, I think I had a foot in each camp. I designed, I liked business, my skills developed with the marketing. I had the contacts to go out and get the work too. When times were hard we called on a lot of people we knew who had worked with us at Pei and Warnecke's."

Despite the economic situation, by the end of the year the firm had 25 employees and was expanding so rapidly that it needed new office space. Other Warnecke alumni soon joined KPF, among them Arthur May and William Louie as design partners, and Robert Cioppa as a management partner. Gene wrote to developers and marketed the company's services aggressively offering feasibility studies and development advice as well as design services. The AT&T office complex in Oakton, Virginia, came as a result of Gene's association with AT&T in Warnecke's office.

"That was a pretty good building, but it took three to four years before we really had our feet on the ground," according to Bill. "Because we were starting with big projects, with almost no staff, projects were coming in over the transom, and we had nobody to do them. It was not like the organization we have today, and it was an extremely, extremely difficult period, but we got ourselves through it."

"The building that brought us to notice was 333 Wacker Drive. That was a wonderful opportunity. It was the point at which we started to gain our confidence. It came as a result of Gene knowing Tom Klutznick in Chicago; and at the beginning of the project ABC television was involved in it too, and that connection came as a result of Shelly Fox who had a very close family connection to Bob Goldman at ABC. We subsequently went on to do a lot of ABC work."

"333 Wacker Drive without question put us on the map," says

6

7

Gene. "But the interview we did with Procter and Gamble, beating I.M. Pei and Skidmore, was a real turning point. The day we learned that we had won is still one of the most exciting days of my career. Procter and Gamble had the longest interview process; it took a year or more. They finally narrowed it down to three, had the interviews and decided to pick us; but they still required the approval of CEO John Smale (who later became head of General Motors) and Brad Butler who was the chairman. Bill and I were asked to fly to Cincinnati and meet them. I can see it now as though it was yesterday. We were both in blue suits and white shirts. We presented. Bill did a great job talking about design. We didn't know how we had done because they kept a very straight face. We were going down the escalator to the street to take a taxi to the airport when Brad Butler comes running up and says "Look, I want you to have a good weekend and a good flight home. You've been selected." Bill and I flew home without the plane! It was a really exciting moment. It was a major job—an 800,000 square-foot new headquarters building and we had just beaten two great firms."

Bill Pedersen recalls that they were fortunate not only to get the job but to work with two people—Smale and Butler—who were not only inspirational individuals but who worked with the architects in a totally focused way.

"When we would have a meeting with them, they would not accept a phone call from their secretaries or anyone." Bill recalls. They were totally focused on what we were doing and talking about. That dynamic produced a good building. The method by which we developed our design process and the manner in which we introduced it to clients was tremendously important. It had its genesis back in the Warnecke days when Gene and I were working on a project up at City College. I came in after having been at I.M. Pei's and I thought "I'll do my great design and sell it to them." Well, I did my great design and I didn't sell it to them at all. It made me realize that we had to find a different way of working. So we started this process that I dubbed the comparative method, where we look at a series of different possibilities. Not with the intention of introducing a long menu and asking the client which one do you want. The idea is to be able to compare one design against the other, so that one can logically explain why one design seems to work for a particular client. And that seemed to work."

"We brought four designs to John Smale, and John said, 'Now that I see these, I can understand what I really want to accomplish. Frankly, I don't think any of the four you presented, while they are interesting, is exactly what I want to do.' He went on to say how he wanted to join the old building and the new building together to create a unified whole. From that comment, which was totally fundamental to the nature of the design, we went back and designed the L-shaped structure that turned out to be a very good building for its particular type and won a National AIA Award. That, to me, is the essence of the way we practice architecture. We hope to get our client involved in such a way that they can make a contribution on the level of understanding their project that we can capitalize on, and that's the way we've worked all along, and I think that particular success with John Smale was the most dramatic evidence of the validity of this comparative process."

"It wasn't about just saying 'That's the most exciting'," adds Kohn. "It was giving them all the issues such as cost, function, delivery, master plan and its relationship with the city. It made them think."

Kohn's genius was in the marketing of the practice. He has been described as the best architectural marketeer in the business and as much thought frequently went into the presentation of the work as into the design solutions themselves.

"We had very creative presentations. We always thought about what clients were looking for, what was special about them and what might appeal to them. We did our research, sometimes to the extreme. On one job, a long time ago, we had pictures of the houses the clients lived in, the cars they drove, how they looked when they dressed, so we could judge their taste level and how to appeal to them. We sometimes misjudged things. We thought that Lutherans didn't drink and so when we had lunch we had no wine. The first thing they asked for was the wine!"

In the early days there was no PowerPoint, and Bill and Gene would do creative slide shows with two projectors. One slide might show a project and the other would show several details relating to that image.

"You could create stories. We always had stories about what we were proposing and why," says Kohn.

The success of the presentations was helped by the chemistry between the two architects.

"That was the beautiful thing. Clients would tell me that our reaction to each other was quite natural. We reinforced each other. We didn't battle or argue. Clients felt that we were a team and the clients were getting the best of the firm and of us. We used humor a lot and were responsive to each other," Kohn continues. "We weren't arrogant. I think they liked us. If clients like you and respect you, and then you do a creative presentation that deals with the issues they are most concerned with, then you will win."

Bill interjects with a story about an interview in Cleveland, Ohio, for a big banking job there for AmeriTrust.

"Very few of our presentations did not begin without a few slides of Gene pitching and me hitting for the softball team. It was a very important part of our office. We were architectural league champions for 5 years in a row. People were coming to work with us because they were not only good architects but also because they played good softball! Gene was a very crafty pitcher and I was a pretty good hitter. When we started the interview, we showed our slides of our softball team; what we didn't know—we hadn't done the research—was that the person who was interviewing us was the owner of the Cleveland Indians baseball team. He really took to us, so we got the job. Harry Cobb of I.M. Pei's office also interviewed for the job. I had a party at my home after we had been awarded the job. Harry asked how the interview went and I told him about the softball team and he looked at me aghast and said 'That's unethical!'"

"He was furious!" Kohn said, chuckling.

8. Goldman Sachs European Headquarters, London, United Kingdom. Kohn Pedersen Fox, 1992.
9. JR Central Towers & Station, Nagoya, Japan. Kohn Pedersen Fox, 2000.

8   9

During the 1980s the firm built a reputation as exponents of Postmodernism, an exuberant, contextual architecture which had a brief flowering. It put KPF on the map architecturally and their PoMo designs were much imitated in the Far East where complete buildings were frequently copied directly from the practice's publications.

"When you went to Hong Kong everyone had KPF's book, loaded with Postmodern designs that they were copying," says Gene.

"The foray into Postmodernism is a cause for sufficient embarrassment on my part as an architect," Bill admits. "It's something I've been trying to live down for 30 years. Nevertheless, it came about with very noble intentions and they weren't all stylistic. We were doing a lot of tall buildings, and their ability to combine with the fabric of the city was a passion of ours. The thought was that the classical language had within it the elements that enabled buildings to combine. All buildings utilize similar elements—they have pediments and entablatures, columns and pilasters. Because the buildings use the same elements, they tend to be able to create a unified whole, even though they are unique individual structures. And so we felt that perhaps that would be a good theme to apply to the tall building and to enable it to have a base, middle, and top. The problem was that we didn't fully understand the inflation of scale. When a building goes to 50 stories, where the model was seven or eight stories, it becomes an entirely different thing. It did not translate well into the larger scale. Secondly, the vision that everybody would adopt a similar point of view and we all would be this harmonious group and generate buildings with common elements, that just isn't part of modern practice. So that was a frustration as well."

"From my perspective, the period of Postmodernism was a consciously intellectual exercise. I was doing a lot of reading on the history of architecture, studying theory with Colin Rowe and people like that, but my own visual sensibility was really not, frankly, comfortable working in this way. I don't think I ever produced buildings that were of the quality of Jim Stirling's great Staatsgalerie building in Stuttgart, for example. He really did something with that particular language. Ironically, we probably got the most journalistic recognition during the period of time when we were doing our worst work, but it's always like that I guess."

"Buildings coming out of the 60s and 70s" Kohn interjects "were largely glass and inexpensive curtain walls. As a result, the idea of using stone and masonry and less glass was welcomed by developers and corporate clients. They seized upon this because it provided identity. Then the styles got carried to an extreme, it's a natural tendency which you see in each generation—by the time the period is over they have been overly detailed and enriched beyond what they should be. It was an interesting time. It wasn't our best work but it opened the door to our best work when we became much more modern."

After a vacation to India in 1985, Pedersen decided that the Postmodern style no longer suited his aesthetic aspirations, and he went back to the simpler architectural forms of 333 Wacker Drive and moved on from there.

"The breakthrough building for me was the DG Bank in Frankfurt," he says. "We were invited by the Dutch pension fund PGGM to compete against several German architects. I developed a strategy of a building of three parts. The first being the core, which acts as a skewer to then join together the two other parts. Each of those parts had a specific role in gesturing to the city. One gestured to the residential community and one gestured to the commercial community. We wanted to find ways in massing the building so that it picked up the various heights around it. We were going to exceed the height limitations in Frankfurt by about 70 meters, so we were looking to create a building that registered the datum of the traditional city, the city of the mid-rise, and finally the higher city. It was a very successful building and we did a whole series after that which developed two parts or three parts together as a gesture to different aspects of the city. That approach worked fine for buildings up to about fifty stories in height, but when you get to the supertall buildings that we've been doing in China, the scale jump is such that you really can't utilize those strategies any longer. Instead you have to enable the building to become much more serene, much more confident, much simpler as a volumetric. And then at the base you can introduce elements that are more connective in their attitude. The Frankfurt building was a huge turning point for me because it came after I'd been teaching at Yale, right after my involvement in the Postmodern movement, and it came at the time of my trip to India when I had time to think about what I was going to do for this competition when I got back. It was, for me, a breakthrough."

But the design process is more than mere inspiration. It is also hard work and firm organization. Unlike many larger firms, which are organized by departments with a design department, production department and construction department, KPF operates as teams so that the team that starts the job finishes the job.

"That allows the process to be a very continuous one where design can be improved as it moves along," says Gene. "It means we don't have to deal with a production group that ignores what the designer may have wanted. It is a much more unifying approach and it allows for the design partners to be participating all the way through, right to the last piece of glass, to the last brick."

KPF buildings continually evolve during the design processes. There is a huge transition from the first initial idea to its ultimate realization.

"We have built up a team of people that are not only exceptionally capable in their own right, but also focused on trying to make contributions at every step of the game to the building as it evolves," says Bill. "That's a key responsibility of anyone who is leading the design process to encourage that sort of contribution from individuals on the team. Because that collective, collaborate process is where a building is really made. I think that this is the reason why we've been successful in executing our buildings with a high level of resolution. They are really well put together, the materials and details are very well considered."

One of the key elements of the practice today is its global reach. With offices in London, Shanghai, Hong Kong, Abu Dhabi and Seoul, the partners rack up phenomenal air miles as they regularly meet up with clients around the world.

"In 1985 I attended a conference where an economist was addressing an audience of bankers and developers, some architects, and saying that if they weren't global by 1990, half would be out of business," Gene explains. "I was convinced he was talking directly to me. I spoke to Shelly and Bill and convinced them of what we needed to do. You have to remember that at the end of the 80s there was a terrible crash—in the whole of the 1990s only one office block was built in New York! So if we had depended on New York for our livelihood back in the 1990s we would have had no work at all. Going global was important. The first step was to go to England where we had won the job to build the Goldman Sachs Headquarters on Fleet Street. Then we won the DG Bank competition and at the same time we were asked by Taisei, a Japanese firm that we had worked with in Chicago, to go to Tokyo and do a competition with them. That didn't happen, but we got selected with their help for the Nagoya Station project which was a five million square-foot project and that opened the door to Asia, because once we got to Japan, then we'd go on to Hong Kong—on the same ticket so to speak! We soon got work in Hong Kong. Today we have worked in over 35 countries, with a staff of people that come from at least 40 countries. So we are truly global."

"Wanting to go global and succeeding globally are two different things," Pedersen adds. "One of the reasons we were successful with our early work in Japan was that we offered a method of working that was so different from anything the clients encountered over there. They found that they were actually able to participate in the process, in contrast to working with many Japanese architects who didn't allow their clients in the process in the same way."

This collaborative approach is something the partners keep returning to as a key differentiator.

"You still have architects today who come in and say 'this is the scheme', but we don't work that way," Gene states. "Allowing the client to participate in the process makes them really a part of it and excited by it. As a result they become much easier to convince of the things that you want because the logic is going to be there. Sometimes, as a result of that process, the client comes up with an idea better than we might have. We're happy about that. We don't say that we have to be the author of every little thing. If the project ends up great because of the teamwork between us and the client, then that's the best. For European and Asian clients that was really unique."

Globalization has played a significant role in creating strength in depth in the practice, because many emissaries have to be sent out into the world and those emissaries have to be able to handle the job. The partners can't be in every country all of the time.

"You have to rely on other people to do it," says Bill. "We discovered some extraordinary talents, some extraordinary entrepreneurship, in people like Paul Katz and Jamie von Klemperer, in what they did and how they went out there and attacked it as an opportunity for themselves. Had we been confined to this little pool in the United States and tried to create a firm that would transition, we'd be tripping over ourselves all the time because you can't offer enough opportunities. Globalism changed all of that for us, and we were very encouraging of people being able to take advantage of these opportunities. They built up constituencies in the office which has led to a natural evolution of leadership here.

"We now have 23 principals total," says Gene. "They're in three groups: the elders, myself, Bill, Bill Louie; the key leaders, Paul and Jamie and one or two others; and a group of younger partners who are on their way up. When we formed in '76 we wanted the firm to succeed beyond our years and it was important to have transition and to find the kind of people who could become the future leaders. In some instances we were wrong. But in Paul and Jamie we have two outstanding architects. I'm confident they will do a great job in leading the firm. Opening a lot of offices can be expensive. We have enjoyed the fact that we haven't had too many offices to manage. We are at a good size at the moment."

Design depends on talent, and it is Gene and Bill's aim to attract, encourage and recognize the most creative talents in the office to ensure the firm maintains its position in the global market.

"The quality of architecture in the world today is increasing exponentially," Bill concludes. "There are so many firms that are doing really extraordinary work. Firms that are contributing to the collective dynamic of architecture in a way that you cannot compare to the 1970s when we started out and there was nothing going on at all. It was really dead. Now the world is just humming with creative potential, and with an acknowledgement of the role of cities and what they can do from a sustainability perspective and a social dynamic. All of this is changing so dramatically. Much of it has to do with the rise of Asia and the region's tremendous inventiveness and dynamism. We have to make sure that the people who lead us in this incredibly competitive marketplace are people of exceptional talent. Growing those people and enabling them to flourish is something that we think about a lot. It's all going to develop into the future as a result of their energies and capabilities."

In Conversation:
Paul Katz & James von Klemperer

With Peter Murray

Though KPF's work has grown to encompass a broad range of commissions, clients, and collaborators around the world, the firm still functions as a highly personal practice. Geographically distinct offices do not operate as independent centers of creation and management, but rather function as extensions of one group of close colleagues. This cohesiveness relies on strong relationships, with links reinforced by frequent travel, shared ideas, and a common sense of shared adventure.

This strategy of global personal interaction is important to KPF's working method and differentiates them from many other larger firms whose international offices operate more unilaterally. It also represents a point in time as practices morph from being exporters of services working internationally to true global networks.

Paul Katz and Jamie von Klemperer maintain close ties with those that commission the firm whether they be in London, Tokyo, Shanghai or New York. This inevitably means a peripatetic lifestyle for the two partners.

"I think people come to us for a boutique experience," says Katz, "despite the fact that we are a large firm we try to create that very personal touch. We have been fortunate in the scale of the projects we get and that there are enough clients who want a high level of service. Very few of our competitors are as intimately involved in projects in various parts of the world as we are."

"Each of our architects is in regular contact with the place where his or her project is sited and has a real experience of that context," adds Jamie. "It brings great benefits in terms of the transfer of knowledge. At KPF there is a constant quest to discover, develop or perfect some aspect of architectural design

that is essential to moving things forward. It would be hard for us to say 'Here's a model of how to do a project.' That sort of model can exist at certain levels of management but it's hard to do in design. Most of the senior people in our offices in Shanghai, Hong Kong, Seoul or London have worked in our New York office. Without that history of close interaction, I think it's very difficult to capture the spirit of common values and goals and excitement that makes you want to be part of a group enterprise."

Paul and Jamie joined KPF at about the same time in 1984 after both training at Princeton University School of Architecture where they studied with Robert Maxwell (who was then Dean of the School), Alan Colquhoun and Anthony Vidler. Colin Rowe's book *Collage City*, written with Fred Koetter and published in 1978, was a key text. The discussions surrounding the influence of history on contemporary urban development and the significance of context and place played a major role in the two young architects' awakening. KPF seemed an opportune place to apply for work with its growing reputation in Postmodern architecture.

"There was a preoccupation at KPF with the meaning of buildings, as well as with the finer points of material texture. We all debated with each other about how the lessons of history could be translated into modern architecture," says Jamie. "The firm also had a well–deserved reputation in the schools as a place where one could learn the more technical side of the craft of building. KPF gave us a great opportunity to learn something new, to experiment, and be surrounded by others who had had similar experiences in school."

At the time, says Paul, "there were two strong forces in

1

2

architectural design and they were pitted against each other. One was Postmodernism and a reawakening of history and understanding of the city, the other was Modernism. The great American Modernists were quite weak in the 1980s and this firm was fresh. Our training was very relevant. Recalling Alan Colquhoun's lecture series about how the city didn't reject modernism but absorbed history really helped us when we went to work in Japan. The firm was very strong at the time in attracting smart people from each of the most reputable architecture schools on the east coast. The first half of the 1980s marked the end of a long tradition of New York architecture: a tradition of the drafting room, the clients and contractors being local, and everything was still made in America. The clients' fathers and grandfathers were developers. You worked late at night and you pinned the drawings up just before the clients walked in. It had been like that for almost 100 years."

"A nice aspect of that period of practice in New York," adds Jamie, "was the sense of community that existed between firms. We had job captains who had come from Marcel Breuer's office, Edward Durrell Stone's, Roche Dinkeloo's and I.M. Pei's. They represented the postwar inheritors of heroic Modernism—you felt you had touched their buildings because you were working with the same guys who had done their flashing details! Even though this was a new firm you felt very much part of that deep New York heritage of the profession. Of course things started to transform with the advent of the computer in the mid to late 1980s. It changed what a young architect could do because, up to that time, a junior architect was in a sense a manual laborer."

Indeed Paul Katz's early work in the office had little to do with Postmodernism and Collage City. "In the 1980s I did a lot of feasibility studies with developers. Somebody would fax over a site somewhere in Manhattan and then the next day you would go over and explain to them what we could do on the site. That way I got a lot of client contact very early in my career, which helped me to read clients very well. It got me to be good at diagnostics, being able to look at a site and immediately see its possibilities and permutations."

Today the firm's staff is made up of international architects from many different countries. Architects often work on projects for their hometown and then return there when the building is done. "It is a big difference from the days when the firm was founded, receiving people from Columbia, The Cooper Union, Harvard, Princeton, Yale and other east coast schools," says von Klemperer. "Now a big proportion of our young graduates are coming from China, Korea and the Middle East, from places where architecture is a vital concern to the broadest scope of society and where there are great projects that are being built. Many initially come to be educated with the intention of returning home. This group provides us with some of our best architects, including some of our partners. Some will return to a local practice in Shanghai, Seoul, Tokyo or Mumbai, where they will work with us on the other side of the table."

"The basis of the firm," adds Paul, "has been to hire the best people we can and then train them. The reason that Jamie and I are in this position is because we have tried to help as many people that are younger than us achieve and aspire to those same goals. Those people are the ones who put us in the position we're in. We believe they will then relate to us in much the same way as we relate to Gene (Kohn) and Bill (Pedersen). It is that multigenerational community which gives us our strength."

"Architects here feel that they are doing the work that they hoped when they first picked up a pencil, opened up a book on Le Corbusier, Frank Lloyd Wright or Mies van der Rohe. It's not that nobody is doing that individual thing or that it is not recognized. We are all doing it. Perhaps the worst crime at KPF is to take credit for something that someone else deserves or should share credit for. That applies to the design culture of the firm as well as to the different generations. We can say to the original owners 'You started it and did all the work, we are just carrying on' and they can say 'Well, we opened the doors, but we wouldn't be anywhere without the efforts of the many people that followed'. We are a little bit like the Chinese government: the older you get, the more you have to contribute and you might not be sitting right at the front row, but at the same time you are just as influential. It's very nice to think that the older partners can continue as long as they care—and they do care—but also know that as a younger participant your career isn't being constrained." This evolving structure of the practice is in part the natural change that occurs with growth and over time, but it has also been accelerated by the internationalization of the practice's workload.

"The globalization of the financial services industry really took us on, rather than us deciding to take it on ourselves," says Paul. "London was first, with the Big Bang, with Goldman Sachs on Fleet Street and the Reichmann's at Canary Wharf in 1987. It was easy to work in London because they spoke English and the architects weren't that well organized. At the same time the biggest investors in global real estate were the Japanese. A lot of our buildings were being sold to them after the 1987 stock market crash. The Japanese came over here with a deep interest in the production of architecture. They were imagining how Tokyo would need to be rebuilt to become a global city. Our first real estate work for Asia was in Japan in 1989." KPF's approach, design as a collaborative process with clients, was a success in Japan.

"We didn't go there to sell the same old product, we went with an open mind," says Katz. "We wanted to learn from Japan and find out what we could improve because of our interaction with the country and its people. I think they were very appreciative of that. We were very lucky; most architects would view Japan as the ideal place to work as the whole culture is built around design. There is nothing you do in Japan that isn't related to design whether it's writing, eating or sleeping. The most basic things are designed. One of the interesting things was that Modernism was never rejected in Japan. Modernism's role after World War II had no pejorative aspect, and when we started working in Japan and dealing with context we were inspired by the Post-Metabolist mind-set that they had. In a way we absorbed that with our understanding of the city that came out of Princeton. The combination of the two helped us to compose and adapt the buildings which we would not have been able to do on our own.

"It's important to remember that adapting buildings to their

2

3

energetic and troubling years of my professional career to date. We had 9/11, two blackouts, we had a transit strike and a ferry crash," Weinshall says. Exhausted by the strains of running the City's transport she sought a change of role and in April 2007 she left the DOT and moved to CUNY.

"There was a lot of planning that was going on and a lot of architects who had been hired to design buildings, but there was no money to finance this. Soon after I started I had to negotiate with the state to create a five-year capital plan. We got $1.6 billion and started about a dozen projects immediately.

"Whether you have a mediocre architect or you have a prominent, internationally known architect you are going to pay the same amount of money for the design. We don't have a disposal strategy. Our buildings go up and they stay there for fifty years. So if a building is going to stay there that long, it's got to be great, dynamic, have a statement. We really do seek design excellence. We are an urban university and half of our campuses are on the city streets. So we are part of the urban framework and we want to have great design and add something to the city."

As Commissioner of the DOT Weinshall had worked with Baruch College when KPF designed The William and Anita Newman Vertical Campus, a 14-story building occupying a full city block in Manhattan's Gramercy Park neighborhood.

"There were a whole bunch of issues regarding the construction of the buildings, so I heard about them. Where I really got to know KPF was with the Advanced Science Research Campus (ASRC) project up at City College. The Chancellor of CUNY has deemed that this is the decade of the sciences and so we have constructed or are in the process of constructing a number of major science complexes. One of his concepts is to create a science research park where all of the campuses could partake in a state-of-the-art research building."

The Advanced Science Research Campus will offer CUNY a new multi-disciplinary academic research facility with laboratories, classrooms, faculty and administrative offices and café. It is part of a traditional campus embedded within the urban context of Manhattan's historic Harlem neighborhood. On an elevated rock outcropping and along St. Nicholas Park, the South Campus benefits from spectacular views in three directions and the ASRC's fluid geometric forms take inspiration from gorge formations in the surrounding landscape. The buildings are designed to accommodate a wide range of research initiatives and will provide laboratories for the more environmentally demanding activities that cannot be accommodated by renovating the existing buildings.

The Advanced Science Research Campus was just beginning when Weinshall started at CUNY and the project immediately hit an issue. The adjacent Structural Biology Center was concerned about the amount of excavation needed and that it would disrupt their sensitive research equipment.

"KPF came up with a brilliant idea that kept the same design but moved them further away from the Center," says Weinshall. "It cost us 18 months and more money because

4

of the delay and design modification to the site but it wasn't astronomical. It was one of those elegant ideas that made us think 'why didn't we think of that before?' So that's where I was first introduced to KPF.

"The project team had some difficulty in convincing the scientists who would occupy the ASRC building to accept the interior design proposals. In the meetings I reiterated that we are a university not a corporation, we can be fun, color can add aspects to a building. After several months of discussions we convinced them and we added some color. I would have to say that in my dealings with KPF on this project they went a long way towards educating the people at ASRC and really added to what is going to be a spectacular building. The KPF team really got to understand the end users of the building, in terms of their philosophy, culture and ideology."

Weinshall has worked closely on ASRC with KPF principal Jill Lerner, who heads up the academic and institutional projects team in the practice. Jill, as President of the New York Chapter of the American Institute of Architects, has made globalism the theme of her term, a decision that highlights the international role not just of KPF but of U.S. practices generally.

"New York is a global city and a global hub for talent, architecture and design, for exporting design services," says Lerner. "Going all over the globe and creating signature buildings, important master plans, exporting values of sustainability of places and pushing the envelope in terms of technology. We should celebrate that.

"KPF are very good team players when working with other firms elsewhere. Many larger firms here spent much of the 90s building around the U.S. and setting up regional offices. We did all our work from New York, so we come to it with a culture of doing a building in Texas, Arizona, Minneapolis, California or Florida where you have to understand not just the climate but also the culture of the place. Those values have helped us expand globally; you come to it with a respect for the environment you are working in and a goal of trying to understand that culture while being able to help shape the aspirations of that client or city in a physical sense. Teamwork, respect for culture, making sure we are working with people who we want to work with, have all contributed to the reasons why we are successful abroad."

One of KPF's longest standing international clients is **William Ko**. As a young architect in the late 1980s, Ko was working on the design of a small hotel in Hong Kong for the developer Hang Lung. Halfway into the project the client decided that he wanted an office building instead and that Ko should work with a practice with more commercial experience. Although at the time KPF had not built in Asia they were well known through publications, and imitations of their distinctive architecture were to be found sprouting up in the emerging cities of the Chinese mainland. Hang Lung invited KPF to work on the project.

"At the time they were relatively new but they did have a good selection of office buildings," says Ko. "What I found interesting, especially in the context of Hong Kong at the time, was the playfulness of the elevation. It was very interesting

4. Plaza 66, Shanghai, China. Kohn Pedersen Fox, 2000. **5.** Riverside 66 Hang Lung Plaza, Tianjin, China. Kohn Pedersen Fox, 2013. **6.** Earl's Court, London, United Kingdom. Kohn Pedersen Fox, 2011.

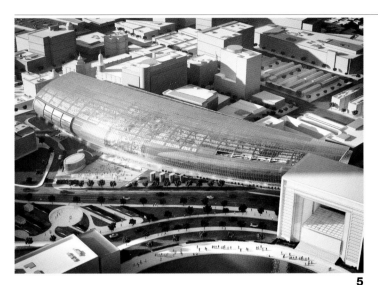

5

6

working with them and it was a good working experience for them as well. There was a different set of rules, different kind of clients that they had to face."

Ko subsequently joined the staff of Hang Lung to work on Plaza 66 in Shanghai, the biggest commercial development the company had done and a flagship development in China because of its prominent location on Nanjing Road. It was therefore decided to hold an international competition and KPF was invited to submit along with four other architects. They were selected for what was to be the practice's first project in mainland China.

The first phase of Plaza 66 was completed in 2000 and soon became a local landmark, with Tower I being one of the tallest buildings in Shanghai at the time, and the low-rise retail frontages onto Nanjing Xi Lu designed to reflect the street context. The office towers, which are set deeper into the site, are punctuated by two major interior public spaces contained by the buildings' curved form. Tower II, completed in 2006, complements Tower I's curvilinear shape, creating a unified composition. Generously landscaped areas buffer Tower II from the residential neighborhood to the north with a screen of planted trees obscuring the parking from the main entry to the building. Similarly, a variety of planted areas soften the edge of the site. The scheme comprises a mix of office, retail, entertainment, and below-grade parking areas and is recognized as the most successful of recent commercial developments in China. Today, Ko is Executive Director of Hang Lung, where he continues to work with KPF on a number of projects in China as well as in Hong Kong.

"I have been working with KPF now for nearly 25 years. When we first started, technology and communications were rather different. A lot of communication was either face to face, which didn't happen very often, or by telephone and fax. Nowadays of course it is easy with video conferencing. The world is getting smaller. In the old days most of their work was produced back in New York whereas now KPF have offices in Shanghai and Hong Kong and work is done in the relevant offices."

Another significant client for KPF in Asia has been Hongkong Land, founded in 1889 the company owns much of Central Hong Kong as well as being major developers and investors throughout the region. Until 2006, **Ian Hawksworth** was executive director of the taipan and hired KPF to carry out commercial projects at a time when there was demand for financial services accommodations.

"It required a steep change from traditional office thinking and as a developer in Asia we needed to have the endorsement of an international architect who had experience in New York, which is where the customer base was being driven," says Hawksworth. "At that point in time American architects weren't working in Asia, there were just domestic Asian architects and some British—who didn't really get it. So we were tapping KPF's expertise in delivering commercial office space."

"Through that relationship we realized that they were a very creative bunch of commercially driven architects. They were designing a product that was functional and essentially sensible which was quite refreshing instead of having a design imposed upon us that didn't work, but the architect loved it!

We got a building which we played a real part in creating and specifying and which ultimately met the occupiers' brief.

"We also found that they were a very efficient young team with the right personal element of being there when they needed to be, both at very senior and more junior levels. The balance of youth and experience was well done. They are a class act."

The success of the relationship meant that Hongkong Land continued to work with KPF on other projects, particularly large-scale buildings in Singapore. Once again KPF's thought-leadership in the commercial market made them a natural choice.

"Singapore was slightly behind Hong Kong at that point, so they were looking at Hong Kong developers to import high grade office accommodation. In that capacity KPF was very helpful in explaining to the authorities the trend in global business as well as global architecture and translating that into a language that the authorities in Singapore understood. That eased the process for us in delivering the type of product that we felt was commercially sensible."

Hongkong Land moved on from offices to more mixed-use projects. The market in Asia was adapting to the power of luxury and challenging the traditional paradigms of how a shopping center might look, not only in its layout but also the form of the shop fronts.

"As there were no real high-quality retail, architects that had a grasp of what was going on globally, I decided that KPF was the right firm to work with. They formed a strong collaboration with other architects that we were using and came up with designs for retail and mixed-use in The Landmark in the center of Hong Kong which has proved very successful."

The Landmark is one of the premier luxury retail centers in Asia. In order to maintain its competitive edge, the complex is regularly updated to ensure that its design and amenities reflect the prevailing retail culture. Phase I of the renovation by KPF involved a complete recladding of the original 1970s building and upgrading internal finishes with French limestone, as well as new storefronts and entrances. Phase II encompasses several components: the addition of York House, a 23-story tower at the corner of Ice House Street; the renovation and expansion of the façade along Queen's Road Central, including the center's new atrium entrance; additional retail space and

restaurants in the new and the existing atria; a boutique hotel (the Landmark Mandarin Oriental) and spa in the lower portion of Edinburgh Tower; double-height storefronts that are part of the flagship retail concept; and a Harvey Nichols department store and a Louis Vuitton superstore on Pedder Street. A suspended, three-story wall of folded vertical glass panels envelopes the new retail podium along Queen's Road Central, unifying the complex's disparate elements.

"We put the design team in front of the brands who were moving into the space and who were very specific about what they wanted," says Hawksworth. "This helped develop the discussions with the brands and create the environment they wanted. In fact, one of the KPF guys ended up as design director for LVMH as a result of the work they were doing for us on The Landmark.

"I would summarize KPF's evolution in Asia as going from just a name that could help us provide the right sort of space for financial services to being recognized as a very creative, collaborative team with a global view. They deliver what the client wants and they work with the end customer to shape their view of what they want. They are always looking ahead, their views based on what they can see in the rest of the world. They do not impose their view of what is currently fashionable which I think can happen with some of the other main players. They are also a collegiate organization and don't mind working with other people. While they are collaborative, they also lead the process.

"In Asia they are probably the highest regarded international architects."

In 2006, when Hawksworth moved to the UK to head up CapCo, owners of the Covent Garden area and developers of the massive Earls Court project, he first hired KPF to help with the upgrading of Covent Garden from tourist honey pot to luxury retail center.

Over the centuries Covent Garden has undergone many transformations. A key objective for the new master plan for the area was to reinvent it as a destination and urban quarter that attracted not only visitors but local workers and residents alike. The success of this strategy was linked to understanding how the public realm —streets and spaces—could reinforce a 're-invented' Covent Garden. The master plan analyzed Covent Garden and its multiple roles as a public space, a place of heritage distinction, and a cultural venue and shopping district at both the metropolitan and local scale. Interventions include streetscape improvements, wayfinding and lighting strategies, landscaping and building redevelopment.

"The approach that KPF has in London reflects their global view, that there may be another way of doing things than the way they have always been done," says Hawksworth. "I think London is ready for some fresh thinking on some of its larger scale projects. Certainly the lessons about retail design we learned together in Asia translate very well to what we are doing with some of our schemes in the UK.

"I like it that they give young guys a lot of responsibility early on so you get real input on what the trends are. The 'new generation' of partners is not that new now of course and they will make sure that the firm continues as a global brand. When Gene and Bill do finally hang up their boots, their greatest achievement will be passing on a culture. That's what makes KPF an interesting outfit to work with."

The new generations have a global view and global experience, which informs work carried out back home. KPF's designs for Hudson Yards would surely be very different if the practice had not worked with large-scale developments in Asia. As the development of Downtown and of Hudson Yards—the "watershed moment" that Chris Ward describes—raises New York's game in the delivery of designs for a 21st-century city, we can see that the impact of globalism on architecture is no longer a matter of merely exporting skills but it is about an exchange of ideas and of learning from different cultures and situations. This reflects a change in relationships in which KPF has been a leading force. There has been a shift from the period when the firm was invited to Asia to deliver skills learned working with New York financial institutions who were themselves seeking suitable office accommodations in the region, as William Ko and Ian Hawksworth have described, to the present day when local offices, staffed by architects from around the globe, provide a contextual understanding supported by the wider practice network. This maturing global vision is a common thread that runs through the projects to be found within this book.

Supertall

Supertall

By William Pedersen

There's something ever egotistical in mountain-tops and towers, and in all of their grand and lofty things.
—Herman Melville, *Moby-Dick*

No building type has generated such fascination and awe as that which we now call the supertall. The dimensional limitations which, only yesterday it seems, defined the outer boundaries of the type have been consistently challenged and surpassed. At a recent conference of the Council for Tall Buildings and Urban Habitat in Seoul, Korea, several projects were presented which dwarfed the 2,600-foot Burj Khalifa. Overcoming nature's limitations has long been a human aspiration and building structures of great height is one of mankind's most visible acts of such striving. However, dimension, whether vertical or horizontal, is never a measure of architectural quality. Architecture, when practiced at its most profound level, is a sublime offering of the human spirit. If we are to build at such a great height much is expected. How are we to meet this challenge?

Several years ago I presented a design to Lee Kai Shing in Hong Kong for a tower located between the Bank of Hong Kong and the Bank of China. My design, which was quite sculptural, was received warmly by him. However, while he felt that it looked to him to be a work of art, he suggested I take it to his feng shui master for an evaluation of the implications generated by the building's form. I did not receive a positive report from the master. He suggested a building which occupies a position between two "warriors" should command that position with serenity and confidence. He even suggested; "with an air of kingly nobility." Translated into more contemporary parlance, one could say that it should play the role of an "urban stabilizer."

I have come to believe that this too is the role of the supertall. Its great bulk and height almost always dwarf the surrounding milieu. Further aggravation of this inevitable scale disparity must be discouraged. To my mind, two design strategies are necessary. First, the role of urban stabilizer must be acknowledged through an external building form which exudes simplicity, serenity and nobility. Secondly, that form ought to be born of a specific connection to the character and culture of the place inhabited. Two supertall buildings, designed by KPF, have been completed and are included in this monograph; The Shanghai World Financial Centre and Hong Kong's International Commerce Center. Have we lived up to our self-imposed expectations?

The Shanghai World Financial Center was started, in design, in 1991 almost twenty years ago. Naïvely, we then talked of it as the world's tallest building. Not so naïvely, we intended to make its design bear the specific influences of the Chinese culture into which it would emerge; but how? Two paths were open to us. We could, as did the designers of the neighboring Jin Mao tower, make it overtly Chinese in its historical allusion. Or, we could take a more abstract tack towards our objective. We chose the latter.

For a remarkably short period of time the Pudong district of Shanghai was the world's largest construction site. Eighty tall buildings, the lowest of which is forty stories, were built within a few years. The frenetic activity of their construction was only matched by the visual cacophony created by the competing aesthetics of their various architectural styles. No urban context cried louder for the presence of a stabilizing and quieting voice, which could bring some semblance of order and tranquility to the surrounding chaos.

It would be trite to suggest that a timeless building was our objective. All buildings are of their time, and only those which represent their era by extraordinary sophistication can achieve the status of timeless. However, one can attempt to create buildings, which, through their form, are less bracketed in time and suggest the infinite. The ancient pyramids are the most obvious examples of this intention. The elementary simplicity of their geometry powerfully acknowledges the poetic duality between earth and sky. No structure, of human creation, more fully dramatizes this dialogue than does the pyramid. However, no structure on earth finds this confrontation, dimensionally, less escapable than does the supertall.

The ancient Chinese represented the earth-sky duality by the juxtaposition of the square and the circle. Comparatively recent excavations of their burial tombs have revealed the placement of two objects accompanying the body of the deceased; a square stone prism and a circular stone disc. The square prism is of dark, representing the earth. The circular disc is light, representing the heavens. We looked to these primary geometries to initiate our investigation into the building's form. Subsequently, the interaction of square and circle formed the basis of our design.

Two program types are included within the body of the SWFC tower; office and hotel. Ideal form for the office type suggests a square with a uniform dimension from core to outside wall. Ideal form for the hotel type suggests a more rectangular shape. We must enable these two types to coexist within the same volume. The manner in which the interaction between

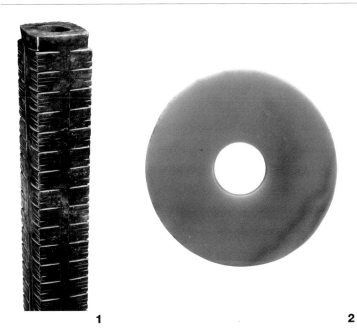

1   **2**   **3**

the two primary geometries of square and circle was developed brought about the formal result. Cylindrical segments of two circular arcs intersect a square prism. The circular arcs generating these cylindrical cutting planes are almost of celestial dimension. The effect of this geometric intersection creates ideal floor configurations for each programmatic type. Program and form are satisfied by a single gesture. While many other aspects of this building are worthy of extended explanation, none are equally fundamental to achieving our stated objective; an urban stabilizer serenely arising from a meaningful cultural connection.

Years later we designed the International Commerce Center (ICC) in Hong Kong. Balanced on the edge of Kowloon's waterfront, the building creates a type of sentinel, marking the entrance, into the inner harbor. From this remarkable vantage point, the entire elevation of central Hong Kong is displayed against a backdrop of verdant mountains. The merger between the city, as a human construction, and the landscape, as a work of nature, is so complete that it takes little imagination to suggest that the tall buildings are themselves a type of vegetation frantically reaching vertically for light and air. Or so it seemed to us, as we searched for a means of joining our new structure into this unique context.

In the vegetable world, a living plant is often sheathed by interlocking layers which enclose the fruit within. To us, the wrapping of an inner realm by light independent layers of enclosure suggested possible avenues of expression, which could make reference to components of Chinese traditional architecture. Firstly, the layers were horizontally serrated to form a series of shingles or scales. The incremental tilting of

the vertical plane towards the sky transforms the quality of light reflected from the surface of the wall. In relationship to other surrounding glass structures it makes a dramatically brighter reflection of light. To local citizens these scales have also suggested another connection. The meaning of the word Kowloon, in Chinese, is nine dragons. To many, the scales refer to the skin of a dragon. A further suggestion of this association comes from the light outer layers as they come to the ground. Since they act with relative independence from the body of the building, they are free to disengage and sweep out to create sheltering canopies above the separate building entrances. The curvature of these canopy forms is clearly suggestive of traditional Chinese roof forms as they hover over the earth. The most dramatic of the canopies extends over the axis of entrance from public transportation and has been dubbed the Dragon Tail.

Since the completion of these two buildings we have been designing tall buildings of even greater height. For these, we are introducing a slight shift in emphasis. While our intentions are still anchored by the two primary concerns of formal nobility and cultural linkage we have begun to explore a heightened interest in the structure's anatomy. Past the height of 1,500 feet, the implications of supertall are fully imposed upon the building's structure. Its biology must be altered. Concurrently, the internal spatial experience can be altered as well. The expression of community made possible by vertical spaces of social exchange point towards the supertall becoming truly a vertical city. All of this leads us to believe that the potential inherent in the building type is just beginning to be realized. The coming years could bring about a golden age for the supertall…and for urbanism.

Shanghai World Financial Center

Shanghai, China

Location	Shanghai, China
Year	2008
Address	100 Century Avenue
	Lujiazui Financial and
	Trade Zone Center
	Pudong District
	Shanghai 200120 China
Size	4,100,000 GSF / 381,600 GSM
Height	1,614 F / 492 M
Program	Office, hotel, restaurant,
	observation deck
Structure	Concrete and steel

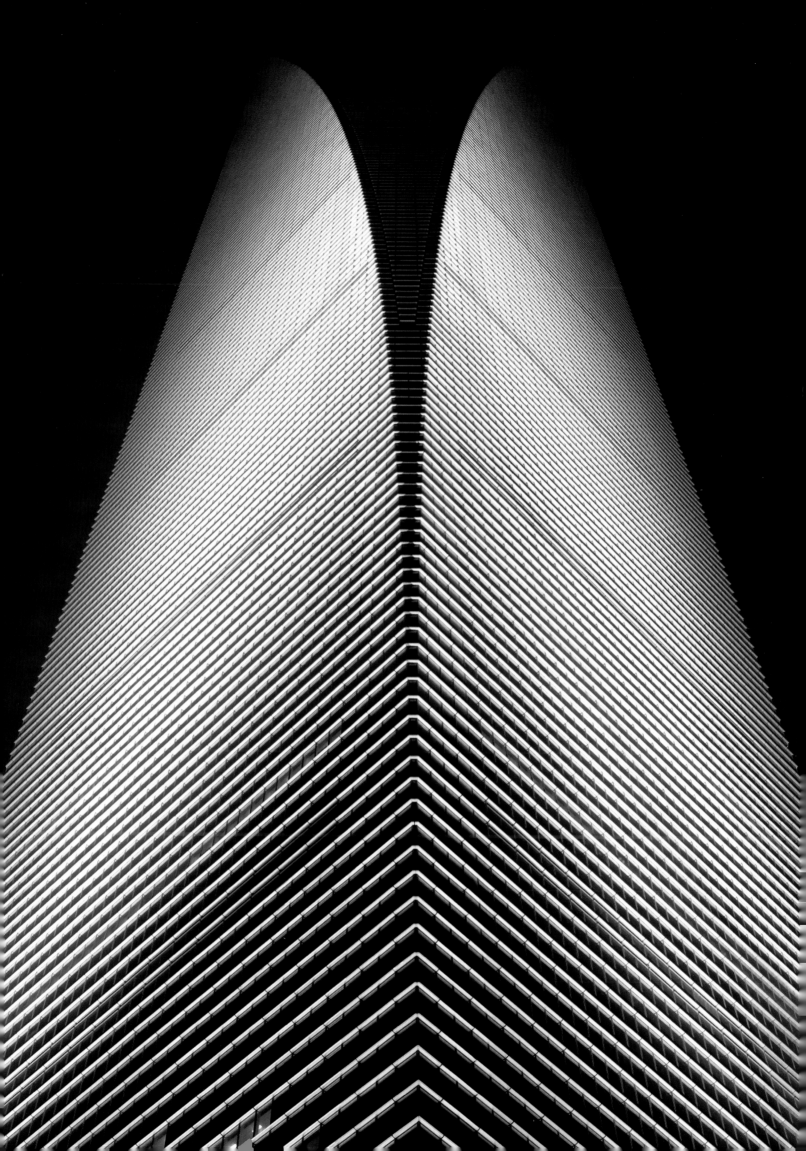

International Commerce Centre

Hong Kong, SAR

Location	Hong Kong, SAR
Year	2011
Address	One Austin Road West
	West Kowloon, Hong Kong, SAR
Size	2,800,000 GSF / 273,000 GSM
Height	1,608 F / 484 M
Program	Office, hotel, restaurant, retail,
	public observation deck, airport rail link
Structure	Composite concrete and
	steel megastructure

Supertall

1

2

1. Tower Section
2. Tower Section

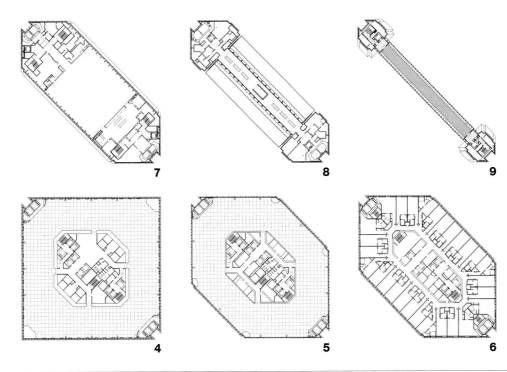

7 8 9

4 5 6

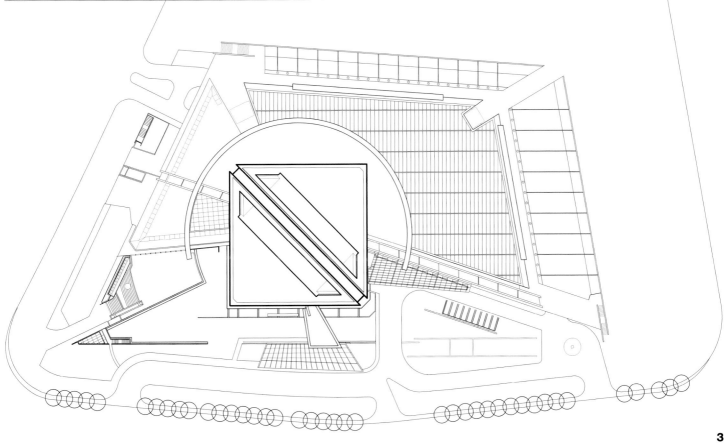

3

4. Office Floor Plan at Lower Levels
5. Office Floor Plan at Upper Levels
6. Typical Hotel Floor Plan

7. Sky Arena Floor Plan
8. Sky Walk 97th Floor Plan
9. Sky Walk 100th Floor Plan

3. Roof Plan

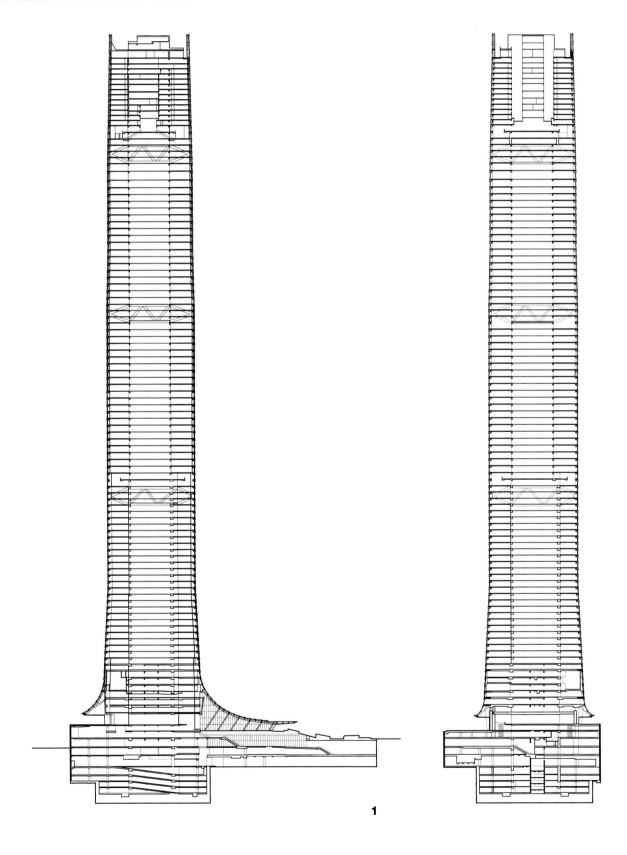

1. Tower Section
2. Tower Section

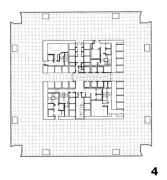

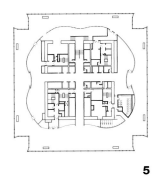

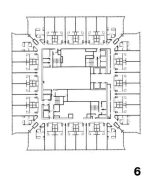

4   **5**   **6**

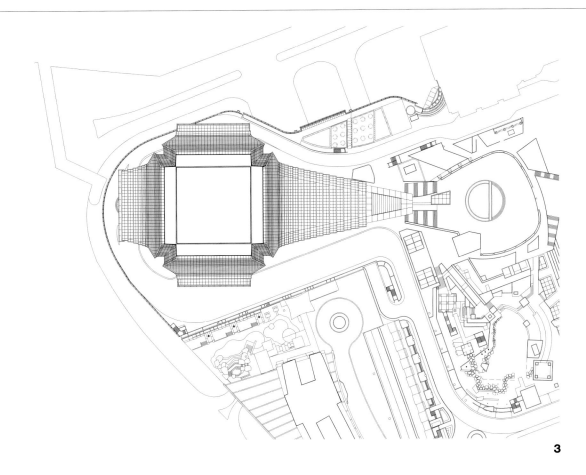

3

4. Typical Office Floor Plan
5. Observation Floor Plan

3. Roof Plan   **6.** Typical Hotel Floor Plan

Endesa Headquarters

Madrid, Spain

Location	Madrid, Spain
Year	2003
Address	60, Calle Ribera Del Loira, Carretera de Accesso al Campo de Las Naciones Madrid 28042 Spain
Size	972,505 GSF / 90,348 GSM
Height	114 F / 35 M
Program	Office
Structure	Concrete and steel

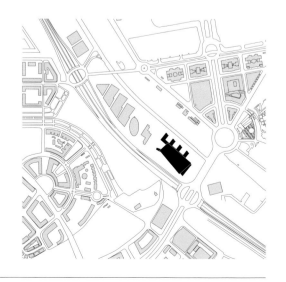

RBC Centre

Toronto, Canada

Location	Toronto, Canada
Year	2009
Address	155 Wellington Street West
	Toronto, Ontario M5J 1A1 Canada
Size	1,400,000 GSF / 135,000 GSM
Height	604 F / 184 M
Program	Office, retail, parking
Structure	Concrete and concrete-encased
	steel columns

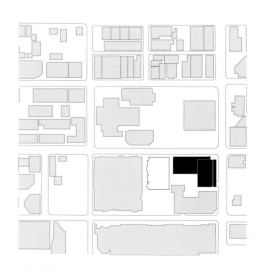

Mirae Asset Tower

Shanghai, China

Location	Shanghai, China
Year	2009
Address	166 Lujiazui Ring Road
	Lujiazui Financial and
	Trade Zone Center
	Pudong Distrct
	Shanghai 200120 China
Size	885,277 GSF / 82,245 GSM
Height	591 F / 180 M
Program	Office
Structure	Concrete with steel crown

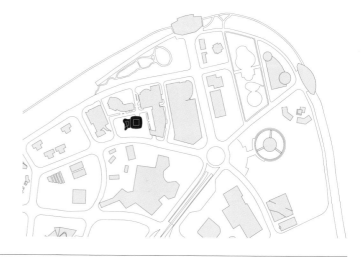

China Huaneng Group Headquarters

Beijing, China

Location	Beijing, China
Year	2010
Address	4 Fu Xing Men Nei Street
	Xicheng District
	Beijing 10031 China
Size	1,400,000 GSF / 130,000 GSM
Height	592 F / 55 M
Program	Office
Structure	Steel reinforced concrete

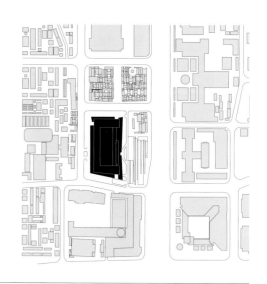

CNOOC Headquarters

Beijing, China

Location	Beijing, China
Year	2006
Address	6 Dongzhimen Outer Alley
	Dong Cheng Qu
	Beijing 100005 China
Size	1,000,000 GSF / 92,903 GSM
Height	292 F / 80 M
Program	Office
Structure	Concrete

Posteel Tower

Seoul, Korea

Location	Seoul, Korea
Year	2002
Address	Yeoksam-dong, 735-3, Gangnam-gu
	Seoul 135-080 Korea
Size	477,000 GSF / 44,314 GSM
Height	436 F / 133 M
Program	Office
Structure	Steel

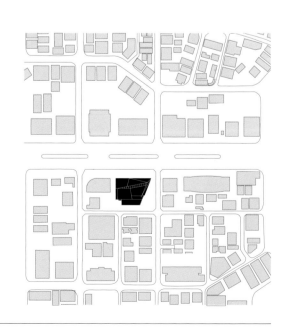

Abu Dhabi Investment Authority Headquarters

Abu Dhabi, United Arab Emirates

Location	Abu Dhabi, United Arab Emirates
Year	2007
Address	211 Corniche Road, PO Box 3600
	Abu Dhabi, United Arab Emirates
Size	939,708 GSF / 87,301 GSM
Height	636 F / 194 M
Program	Office
Structure	Concrete

CNOOC Headquarters

2

1

1. Ground Floor Plan
2. Typical Office Floor Plan

Education
& Research

Education & Research

By Jill N. Lerner

The history of great institutions is tightly bound with their specific place and the buildings that embody their mission, and academic campuses participate in forging the student experience for a lifetime. What would Stanford be without Memorial Hall, Harvard without Harvard Yard, Cornell without its scenic gorges, or Kahn's great Salk Institute without its Pacific views? For students, faculty, researchers and visitors, the physical environment should be a place of intense intellectual engagement and inspiration. Our role, as architects, is to shape and define a memorable experience, to design buildings that serve immediate pedagogical and cultural needs, and to make a permanent contribution to a campus or institution over the long term.

In each specific plan or building the goals of our institutional work have been consistent with KPF's guiding philosophy: to create a design that addresses its specific context and climate, one that meets the functional needs and requirements of the program or brief, and to develop a design expression that aligns with the owner's and users' aspirations. Each building is a unique response to its context; and each is also directly connected to the mission of the institution.

In our recent work the Chapman Graduate School of Business for Florida International University (FIU) in Miami and the Ross School of Business in Michigan demonstrate that difference. Each has a vastly different expression, utilizing distinct materials and planning principles appropriate to their mission, campus and environment. One is sculpted using precast concrete and color that evokes the institution's many Hispanic references as the academic link between North and South America; the other utilizes terra cotta and stone, acknowledging the campus's natural materials and warm color palette, with a signature interior space appropriate to its northern climate.

Nonetheless, in both projects the key planning strategies are similar, with a focus on creating an active campus center, bringing together the student and faculty communities and broadening outreach. Ross does this by its dramatic central

winter garden, essentially creating a living room where students, staff and faculty can and do meet; FIU accomplishes the same goals with its exterior, landscaped courtyard, designed to capture breezes and provide shade in this tropical environment. Both projects provide spaces of varied scales to allow a range of activities from quiet, individual and group study to major gatherings and public events.

What is taught in these buildings may change over many decades, but the exterior envelope, the massing, the key public spaces and major circulation will most likely remain for fifty, or even one hundred years or more. Key to their success will be the quality of construction, durability of materials, and flexibility to gracefully incorporate change over time. Gateway projects such as the Science Teaching Student Services Center at the University of Minnesota address the larger civic community with a dominant presence at the front door of the university while maintaining a dual expression, addressing two distinct contexts, the river vs. the campus. In providing an active, pedestrian street life and clear and inviting entries, it contributes to its campus at multiple levels; scale plays a major role, engaging the local context and contributing to a welcoming campus environment.

As our work has progressed from academic to medical and research projects, and from individual buildings to campuses or precincts, each step has allowed us to expand our knowledge and expertise. All are intensely program-driven problems and are, accordingly, designed both from the "inside out," and from the "outside in." Our most successful projects go beyond internal room-by-room space requirements in order to transform the culture and affect behavior in positive and meaningful ways. From programming to design to execution, we interpret internal requirements in ways that may encourage dynamic learning both within and beyond the classroom, and provide research environments that promote increased collaboration among participants. Inside and out, it is the attention to detail, the use of materials, and incorporation of natural light and public art that all contribute to the spirit of our academic work.

1

2

3

4

Clients for these projects have many decision-makers and multiple stakeholders. Often everyone has input into the design—faculty, students, staff, administrators; donors and alumni; funding agencies, community groups, and even taxpayers. Over the years we have learned from leaders in academia, in research, or in medicine about the future aspirations for their programs and institutions. Our clients have consistently challenged our thinking but supported the creativity of our solutions. Often they become enthusiastic advocates of the power of architecture to transform campus experience or even the institutional culture.

Comparing multiple schemes allows one to more easily engage stakeholders, and this process has informed our exploration of these building types. Input from many directions could result in watered down design, a simplistic recreation of the past, or a building oriented toward the lowest common denominator with little architectural consequence. Rather we choose to view multiple inputs as an opportunity to better understand the building's numerous audiences. Addressing multiple perspectives in our process creates a rich overlay of ideas from which a great solution can be derived.

Ultimately, academic buildings have a real responsibility to inspire new thinking and to foster direct dialog and exchange, capitalizing on face-to-face interaction. Research, medical and academic buildings must embrace the notion that rapidly changing technology will require adjusting our fundamental design assumptions in ways we cannot even envision. Study habits, distance learning, medical simulation, research equipment—all will continue to impact the use and configuration of our buildings in the coming years.

Some have asked if the academic campus will still even be necessary in the future. But despite the promise of technology, there is no substitute for personal interaction in a real campus setting. The blend of program, planning and architecture must serve to inspire the building's users with elegant and functional solutions that make human interaction even easier and more important, personalizing the way people work, study, meet and exchange ideas.

As we move toward our third decade of work with varied institutions we continue to expand our work, both geographically and in diversity of project types. New projects for the School of Transnational Law for Peking University in Shenzhen, China; in neuroscience and human behavior at the Semel Institute at UCLA; and at NYU's first urban campus in Shanghai are all based on the principles our practice has developed over time, and point to a wider, more robust and varied practice in the future. In this age of globalization American universities seek to engage the world more fully and directly, while universities worldwide share the aspiration to work to a high bar for academic standards, user satisfaction, and quality of student life. The role of the built environment to foster cultural connections and intellectual exchange is more critical now then ever before. New and special design challenges lie ahead. Our goal is to create campus environments that enable students to learn effectively across cultural borders, in buildings that inspire the next generation of great thinkers and leaders worldwide.

Stephen M. Ross School of Business
University of Michigan

Ann Arbor, USA

Location	Ann Arbor, USA
Year	2009
Address	701 Tappan Street
	Ann Arbor, Michigan 48109 USA
Size	280,000 GSF / 26,000 GSM
Height	105 F / 32 M
Program	Classrooms, faculty and administrative
	offices, conference and meeting rooms,
	auditorium, winter garden
Structure	Steel

Science Teaching and Student Services Center University of Minnesota

Minneapolis, USA

Location	Minneapolis, USA
Year	2010
Address	222 Pleasant Street Southwest
	Minneapolis, Minnesota 55455 USA
Size	115,000 GSF / 10,000 GSM
Height	107 F / 33 M
Program	Classrooms (science teaching, active
	learning, traditionally tiered), student
	services center, offices, student study
	and social areas
Structure	Concrete

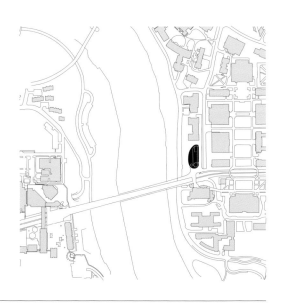

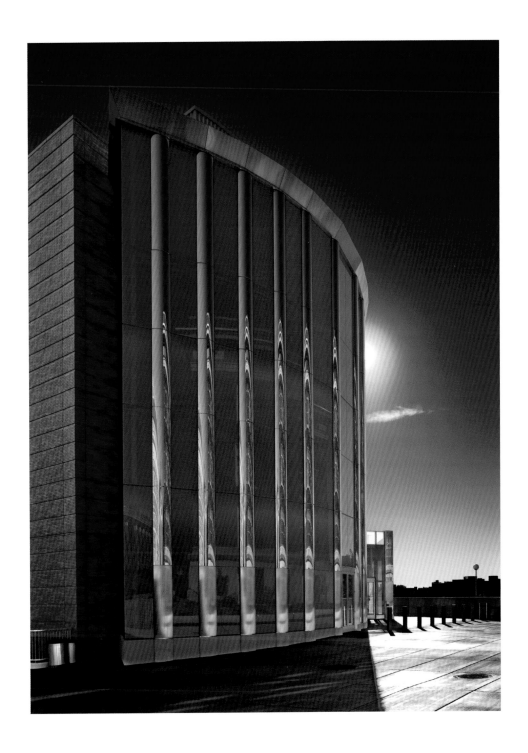

Alvah H. Chapman Jr.
Graduate School of Business
Florida International University

Miami, USA

Location	Miami, USA
Year	2007
Address	11200 SW Eighth Street
	Miami, Florida 33199 USA
Size	92,000 GSF / 9,000 GSM
Height	51 F / 15 M
Program	Classrooms, faculty and administrative
	offices, conference rooms and meeting
	spaces, auditorium
Structure	Concrete

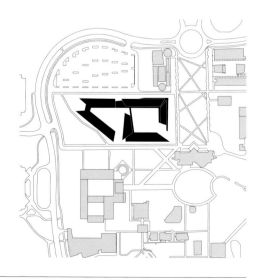

Prince's Gardens Redevelopment
Imperial College

London, United Kingdom

Location	London, United Kingdom
Year	2009
Address	Exhibition Road
	London, SW7 2AZ United Kingdom
Size	344,000 GSF / 32,000 GSM
Program	Student housing, dining
Structure	Concrete and steel

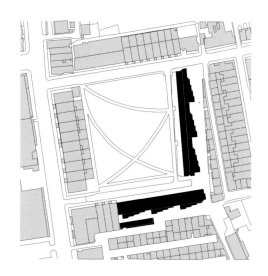

Chadwick International School

Incheon, Korea

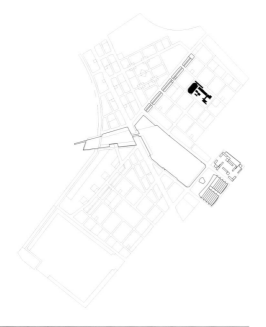

Location	Incheon, Korea
Year	2010
Address	17-4 Songdo-dong, Yeonsu-gu
	Incheon, Korea
Size	506,000 GSF / 47,000 GSM
Height	82 F / 25 M
Program	Classrooms (K–12), offices, media center,
	arts and athletic facilities, cafeteria
Structure	Concrete

INCS Zero Factory

Nagano, Japan

Location	Nagano, Japan
Year	2008
Address	Kanazawa 3410-5, Chino-Shi
	Nagano, Japan
Size	86,000 GSF / 8,000 GSM
Height	34 F / 10 M
Program	Office, factory
Structure	Concrete and steel

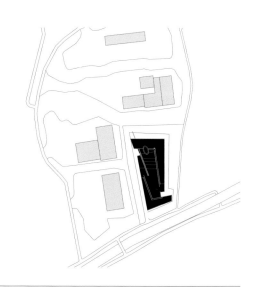

Education & Research

Stephen M. Ross School of Business
University of Michigan

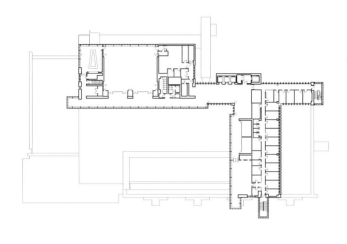

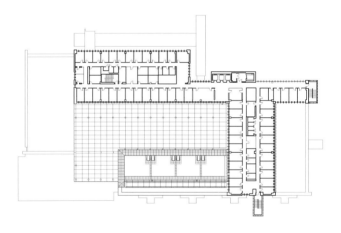

3

2

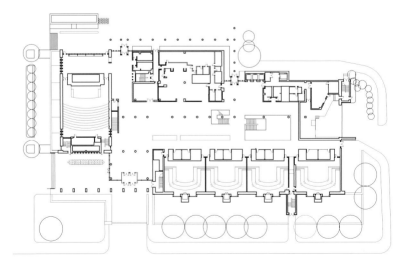

1

1. Ground Floor Plan
2. Fourth Floor Plan
3. Sixth Floor Plan

Science Teaching & Student Services Center
University of Minnesota

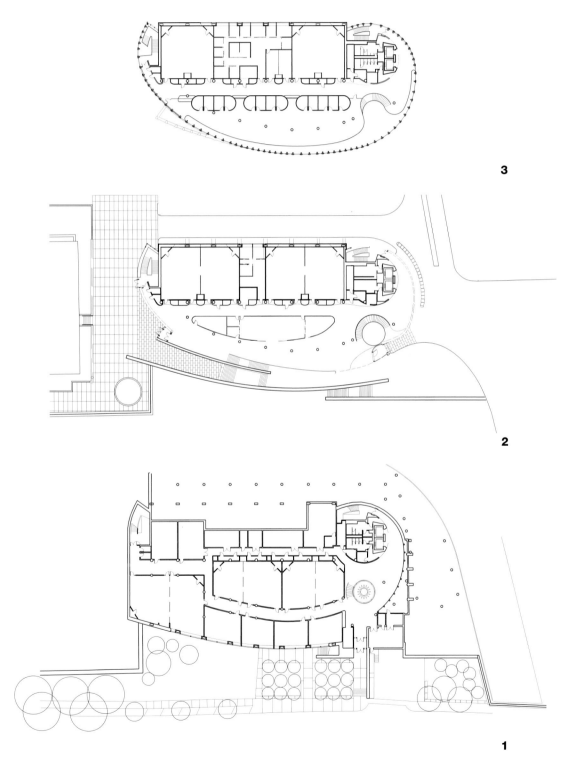

1. First Floor Plan, East River Road Level
2. Third Floor Plan
3. Fifth Floor Plan

Alvah H. Chapman Jr. Graduate School of Business
Florida International University

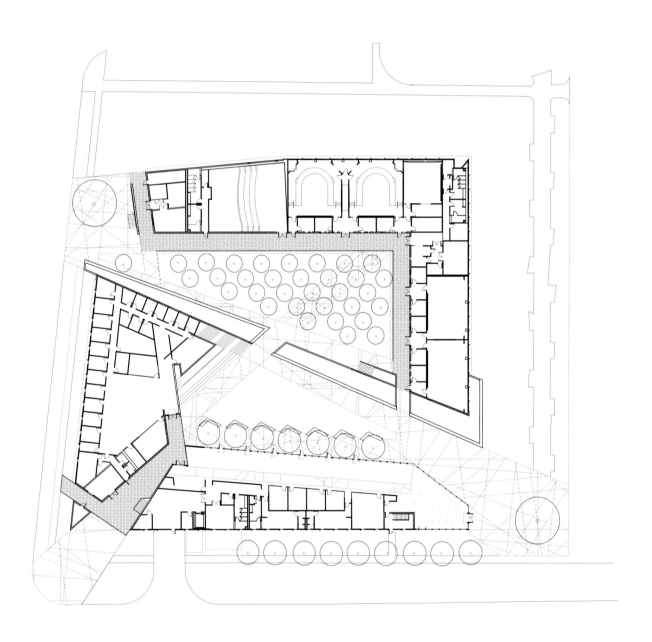

1. Ground Floor Plan

Chadwick International School

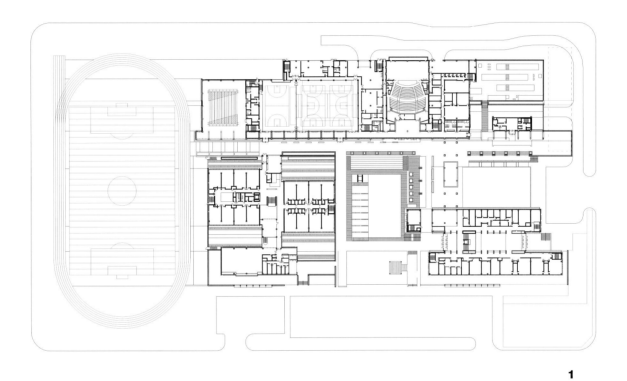

1

1. Ground Floor Plan

Office Buildings

Office Buildings

By A. Eugene Kohn

1

When I was a student at Penn in the 1950s, the predominant belief was that office buildings weren't architecture because the same floor configuration was stacked over and over again. The feeling was that such a composition didn't make space and didn't create a place. Architects preferred to design houses, schools, museums, and hospitals—buildings that had a variety of uses. The office building —a relatively young building typology—was typically analyzed based on statistics such as size, leasing depths, number of floors, cost, and return-per-square-foot. The office buildings of the 1950s, 60s and 70s were viewed as real estate, and not architecture.
As cities grew, however, it became clear that the office building could play a key role in the making of urban spaces, and therefore that the quality of these buildings was critically important. Most importantly, an understanding began to emerge that there were different types of office buildings— that a low-rise suburban office building was different from a mid- or high-rise urban tower. There were speculative buildings created to lease to multiple firms as well as corporate headquarters intended as sole homes for companies. Each type of building in an individual urban context yielded a different form or character.

Simultaneously, architects began to reemphasize design in the workplace. Many people spend from eight to ten hours a day in office buildings. The value of properly designed work spaces for these office workers became increasingly important as people spent longer and longer hours in these buildings. Office amenities like food services, health club facilities, breakout space, relaxed meeting areas, and adjoining retail or cultural activities all directly affected the value of a building. The place

of work—and the spatial and social environment it fostered— was key to the success of the building.

When KPF was founded in 1976, Bill Pedersen, Shelly Fox and I realized that many leading architects were not as focused on the urban office building as they were on residential, cultural and educational facilities. No one had yet solved the problem of how these buildings met the ground, how they related to each other (and created vibrant street walls), or how they met the sky and affected the iconography of a city. More importantly, many architects and developers did not seem to realize the enormous impact that these buildings made on people. Whether it was the internal environment or the exterior façade and massing, we could help shape designs that had real and lasting impacts on cities.

We concentrated our efforts on the execution of a number of different types of office buildings. We designed and built urban office towers like 333 Wacker Drive; and we crafted low, three-to-five story buildings for AT&T, IBM and Gannet. Each time, we instilled the buildings with individual characteristics that responded to the client, program and site. We were conscious of adding value through design.

We approached speculative buildings with the same energy as we did when developing corporate headquarters. Despite the fact that speculative office buildings were perceived as anonymous by many architects (because they had to appeal to as many potential tenants as possible) the challenges of building sites, zoning limitations, and budget all contributed to unique design opportunities for KPF. Some of the projects

1. IBM World Headquarters, Armonk, NY. Kohn Pedersen Fox, 1997. **2.** 333 Wacker Drive, Chicago, IL. Kohn Pedersen Fox, 1983. **3.** KPMG European Headquarters, London, United Kingdom. Kohn Pedersen Fox, 2009. **4.** Ping An International Finance Center, Shenzhen, China. Kohn Pedersen Fox, 2017.

2   3   4

featured in this book—505 Fifth Avenue, in New York City, and 555 Mission Street, in San Francisco—were crafted with this kind of individual response to site, context and market. These buildings nestled into their urban context, proving that well-designed speculative office buildings could activate the city and serve as drivers for ongoing urban growth.

As our portfolio grew, so too did the number of cities we worked in. We have designed buildings in New York, Boston, Chicago, Philadelphia, Washington, D.C., Los Angeles, and San Francisco. Since 1988, in cities throughout the world—in London, Frankfurt, Shanghai, Hong Kong, Tokyo, Beijing and Singapore—we have designed office buildings of significance. Buildings like NEATT, in Seoul, or Nihonbashi, in Tokyo, leveraged the expertise we had built domestically in settings further and further afield. Each time, we focused on the individual design response, and on the quality of spaces and impact on the surrounding context. We learned —and eventually mastered—the unique attributes of office environments in each distinct culture. Things like leasing depths, lobby sizes, core configurations and the importance of daylighting in office design all factored in to the kind of buildings we built in each country.

Our work led trends in office design. More and more, we supplemented office space with retail and other programs that helped create twenty-four hour life along streets and within the work environment. In some cases, this was a simple café, in others it included connections to entire retail developments. Office towers like Plaza 66 in Shanghai helped drive the success of these retail destinations and they activated nearby streets

radically transforming neighborhoods. Other examples of such mixed-use buildings are: Roppongi Hills, in Tokyo; Shanghai World Financial Center, in Shanghai; International Commerce Centre, in Hong Kong; DZ Bank, in Frankfurt; and Heron Tower, in London. There are a number of office buildings currently on our boards that will further evolve the typology.

With each design, KPF has always endeavored to push the building type beyond the preconceptions I encountered in school in the 1950s. We have contributed not only to the street life, to the public spaces and public realm of many global cities, but also to their skylines and civic identity. We believe we have helped the profession of architecture see these buildings as vital components of successful and healthy cities, and that our contribution to the lives of the thousands of people who inhabit our buildings has been positive and lasting.

Heron Tower

London, United Kingdom

Location	London, United Kingdom
Year	2011
Address	110 Bishopsgate
	London EC4N 4AY United Kingdom
Size	751,256 GSF / 69,794 GSM
Height	663 F / 202 M
Program	Office, restaurant
Structure	Steel

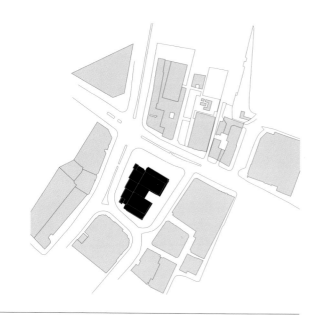

505 Fifth Avenue

New York, USA

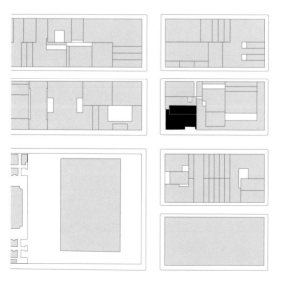

Location	New York, USA
Year	2005
Address	505 Fifth Avenue
	New York, New York 10017 USA
Size	298,000 GSF / 28,000 GSM
Height	311 F / 94 M
Program	Office, retail
Structure	Concrete

555 Mission Street

San Francisco, USA

Location	San Francisco, USA
Year	2009
Address	555 Mission Street
	San Francisco, California 94105 USA
Size	550,000 GSF / 51,000 GSM
Height	487 F / 148 M
Program	Office, retail
Structure	Steel

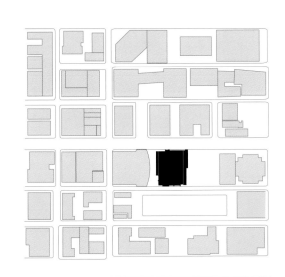

Infinity Tower

São Paulo, Brazil

Location	São Paulo, Brazil
Year	2012
Address	Rua Leopoldo Couto Magalhães Junior
	São Paulo, Brazil
Size	388,000 GSF / 36,000 GSM
Height	387 F / 118 M
Program	Office, retail
Structure	Concrete

Nihonbashi 1-Chome

Tokyo, Japan

Location	Tokyo, Japan
Year	2004
Address	4-6-1, 1-Chome
	Nihonbashi, Chuo-ku
	Tokyo, Japan
Size	983,000 GSF / 91,000 GSM
Height	397 F / 121 M
Program	Office, retail
Structure	Steel

Wheelock Square

Shanghai, China

Location	Shanghai, China
Year	2010
Address	1717 West Nanjing Road
	Jingan District, Puxi (West)
	Shanghai 200040 China
Size	1,200,000 GSF / 114,075 GSM
Height	951 F / 290 M
Program	Office, retail
Structure	Concrete

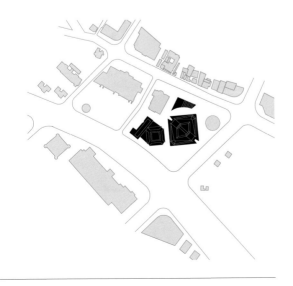

Plaza 66

Shanghai, China

Location	Shanghai, China
Year	2007
Address	1266 Nanjing Road, Hang Lung Plaza
	Nanjing Xi Lu, Puxi (West)
	Shanghai 200040 China
Size	840,000 GSF / 78,000 GSM
Height	731 F / 223 M
Program	Office, retail
Structure	Steel reinforced concrete

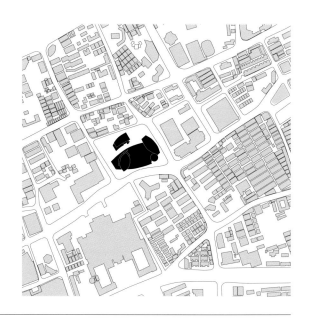

CSCEC Tower

Shanghai, China

Location	Shanghai, China
Year	2008
Address	1588 Century Avenue
	Lujiazui Financial and
	Trade Zone Center
	Pudong District
	Shanghai 200122 China
Size	1,000,000 GSF / 96,655 GSM
Height	544 F / 166 M
Program	Office
Structure	Steel reinforced concrete with
	steel truss crown

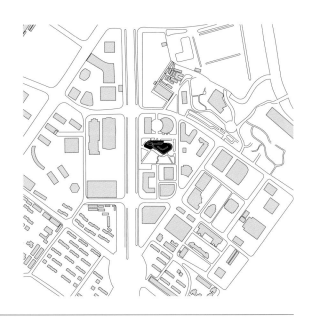

Nihonbashi 1-Chome

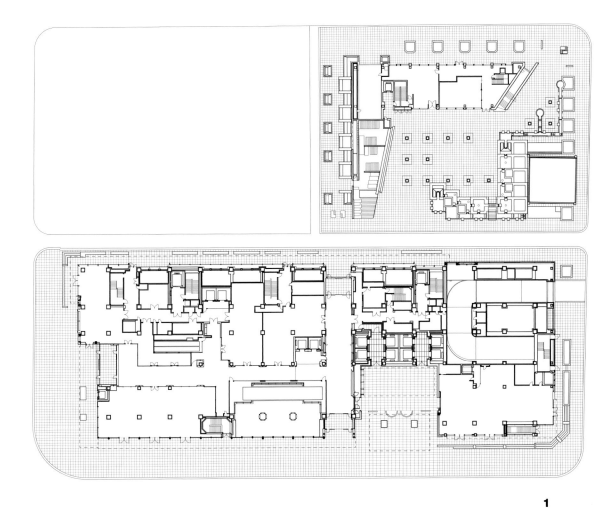

2

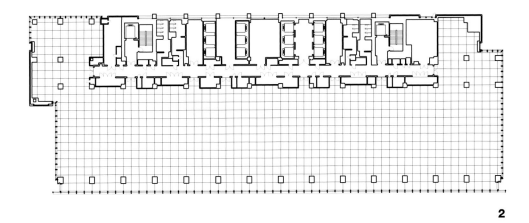

1

1. Ground Floor Plan
2. Typical Office Floor Plan

Repositioning

Repositioning

By John Bushell

There were gasps of surprise when Unilever staff went back into a transformed 100 Victoria Embankment, their global headquarters. A mixture of historic renewal and complete reinvention give the building an unexpectedly vigorous new life, and is an exemplar of our ambition to make meaningful, lasting interventions into existing buildings. We hope to re-position these buildings in the imagination, and in the market.

When the Unilever Headquarters was opened in 1931 it was heralded as a thoroughly "Modern miracle" and indeed there are many innovations in its structure and services that were forward-looking and stand scrutiny today. Unilever simply asked if it was fit for purpose for a 21st Century company—keen to retain its traditional association with the site but only if its operation vigour and the long term value of the building were maintained and enhanced.

We needed to arrive at a view of what continued to perform in today's eyes—our redefined "modern;" what was of value objectively and subjectively, what needed to change and what was the potential of the existing building in comparison with a new one? Are the architectural vision, the spaces created, and the fabric it was realized in still successful? Can the building, if modified, have an uncompromised new generation of life? These are questions that have concerned us over many years and arguably are becoming increasingly important, both to the preservation of layers of memory in the fabric of our changing cities, but also as the careful use of embodied carbon and materials takes on increased significance.

A fascination with the appropriate use of what is already on the site informed KPF's winning competition entry for The World Bank in Washington DC in 1997 where we retained two buildings and evolved a new counterpart to these to form a final cohesive whole around an active covered courtyard space. We have continued a journey to discover how to transform buildings, with very different approaches—from the extension and assimilation in Washington and the internal surprises of Unilever, to weaving new spaces and fabric around the unpromising towers and podiums of the 1970s in Amsterdam and London, the extension and recladding of towers in Paris and New York, and the ingenious reinvention of apparently limited structures in London and New York.

Common to both transformation and new build projects within KPF is the need for thorough analysis and research. A detailed forensic process is needed to understand the original intent and the layers of subsequent modification—what is good and bad about the building from different viewpoints, now, when it was originally conceived and what it may need to do in the future. What of the original is still strong, what needs to be changed? As one goes through this process, a pattern emerges of which era's buildings are capable of easier, greater adaptation. Even within the Twentieth century there is a huge variety. For instance, many of the imposing stone and brick structures of the 1930s are flexible steel frame buildings with stability coming from the mass of envelope construction rather than strictly from "cores," much easier to modify than the bespoke concrete of the 1950s. One can almost go on a parallel process of design element by element, era by era, tracking the combination of architectural intent or ideology, and prosaic

1

2

3

code parameters that produce each period of building elements with their interests, strengths and weaknesses.

Guiding the analysis is a balance between what is there, and the potential for the existing to be used more intensely—whether literally reflecting trends in density of use, reduction in energy use, or more importantly in more diverse patterns of use and an improved internal environment. A puzzle of existing elements and new intentions needs to be worked through.

In preparation to reuse a building, a key element to understand is the strength of the building—the robustness of the structure and foundations. Governing codes and prevalent working practices have a great influence—with several "watershed" Building Code moments defining step changes in the characteristics and likely reuse potential for structures—great underused strength in the late 60s and early 70s gives way to a weaker precision of new codes, decades oscillate between steel and concrete. Below ground, the benefits of leaving the relics of the past undisturbed are complicated by uncertainty of previous construction and current performance. In the structure, a keen sense of architectural history and detailed scrutiny helps inform and evolve an appropriate approach to the transformation.

Whilst more likely to need replacement, the services systems and envelope need the same process of individual scrutiny and assessment. However, while this provides a complex puzzle of parameters and aspirations, the unreasonable magic that creates transformation still primarily resides in the architectural spatial and material intent—made all the

more interesting as it represents a renewed vision of what is appropriate, overlaid on an existing vision. And it is this density of layers and respectful renewal that makes the transformation of the existing building such a rewarding and important contribution to the city.

Unilever London Headquarters

London, United Kingdom

Location	London, United Kingdom
Year	2007
Address	100 Victoria Embankment
	London EC4P 4BQ United Kingdom
Size	392,301 GSF / 36,466 GSM
Program	Office
Structure	Concrete and steel

Tour First

Paris, France

Location	Paris, France
Year	2011
Address	Place des Saisons
	Courbevoie – La Défense 1
	Hauts-de-Seine
	Paris 92200 France
Size	935,000 GSF / 87,000 GSM
Height	Existing building: 515 F / 157 M
	Renovated building: 757 F / 231 M
Program	Office, restaurant
Structure	Concrete and steel

Centra Metropark

Iselin, USA

Location	Iselin, USA
Year	2011
Address	186 Wood Avenue South
	Iselin, New Jersey 08830 USA
Size	110,000 GSF / 10,000 GSM
Height	53 F / 16 M
Program	Office
Structure	Existing and new steel frame,
	cast-in-place concrete slab
	on steel decking

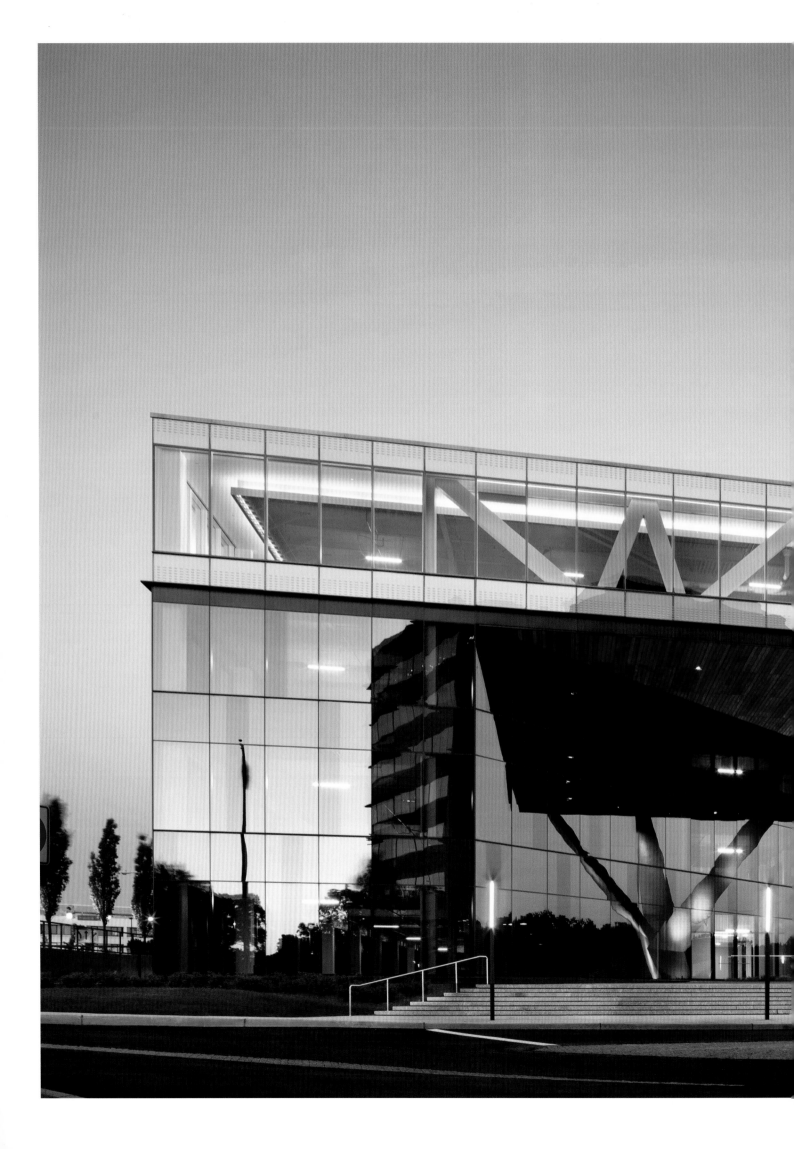

640 Fifth Avenue

New York, USA

Location	New York, USA
Year	2004
Address	640 Fifth Avenue
	New York, New York 10111 USA
Size	302,000 GSF / 28,050 GSM
Height	301 F / 92 M
Program	Office
Structure	Concrete and steel

The Landmark

Hong Kong, SAR

Location	Hong Kong, SAR
Year	2007
Address	15 Queens Road Central
	Hong Kong, SAR
Size	200,000 GSF / 19,000 GSM
Height	377 F / 115 M
Program	Hotel, retail, restaurant, office
Structure	Concrete and steel

World Trade Center

Amsterdam, Netherlands

Location	Amsterdam, Netherlands
Year	2004
Address	Strawinskylaan 1
	Amsterdam 1077 XW Netherlands
Size	1,600,000 GSF / 145,000 GSM
Height	223 F / 68 M
Program	Office, retail, public plaza,
	transit connection
Structure	Concrete with steel roof structure

Children's Hospital of Philadelphia

Philadelphia, USA

Location	Philadelphia, USA
Year	2006
Address	34th Street & Civic Center Boulevard
	Philadelphia, Pennsylvania 19104 USA
Size	792,000 GSF / 73,576 GSM
Height	140 F / 43 M
Program	Emergency department,
	inpatient bed units, cafeteria
Structure	Steel

Hospitality & Residential

Hospitality & Residential

By Joshua Chaiken

KPF's body of hospitality and residential work has a number of distinct roots. Many of the themes in our hospitality and residential work can be traced back to the Roppongi Hills project for Mori Building Company in Tokyo. With this project we experienced a kind of breakthrough in our approach to mixed-use projects. Roppongi Hills demonstrated that these developments could operate both as self-contained cities within cities and as integral parts of the larger urban context. Mr. Mori's sophisticated understanding of this project type embraced the complex relationships that generate successful urban interventions. He selected a great location and conceived a diverse and balanced program mix, but at the same time Mr. Mori also understood that he needed the right team of consultants, operators and other stake holders to properly develop each part and navigate their complex relationships. In this case the Hyatt Corporation was selected to operate the hotel and proved to be highly sympathetic to Mr. Mori's ambitions. Hyatt's goal was to make their hotel an integral component of Roppongi Hills' urban life while maintaining their own identity within this setting. To this end, the food and beverage outlets were one of the key intermediaries. The restaurants on the podium rooftop were made accessible both internally from the hotel as well as externally from the adjacent multi-story shopping mall. The hotel also engages street level activity with café seating flanking the primary vehicular drop-off.

Unlike the initial grouping of buildings at Rockefeller Center, Mr. Mori wanted each building in his development to express their own unique identity while still relating to the whole. To this end we created a hotel design with a warm palette and a modular expression that looks like a hotel and contrasts to the adjacent office tower (also designed by KPF) and the other surrounding buildings. The hotel's exterior character was also informed by a close interface with the interior designers. Peter Remedios' lobby palette and design motifs spill out into the drop-off and he brought some of our exterior materials and geometry inside. This multiplicity of design influences and emphasis on collaboration had an enormous impact on our work.

The evolution of these ideas can be seen in the Xintiandi Hotels. With this project the modular expression of the hotel program was transformed into a patterned wall reminiscent of a Chinese screen rendered in stone. The distinctive wall motif was supported by the client group, Leo Koguan and Shui On Properties, who wanted these hotels to have a strong cultural identity as well as a clear contextual connection to the neighborhood's 1920s masonry architecture. In fact the low rise blocks to the south of these two sites comprise a vibrant retail development with outdoor public spaces, café seating and upscale retail. Again we wanted the hotel program and architecture to engage with this street level energy and pedestrian scale. As such, a layer of two- and three-story retail structures line the south side of our site facing the Xintiandi retail block. The public space behind the two-story structures is both a continuation of the pedestrian retail realm across the street and an outdoor space dedicated to hotel uses.

This understanding of a hotel as a public program actively engaged in shaping the city—started at Roppongi Hills, and furthered in the design of our Xintiandi Hotels—is present in many of our more recent projects. Hotels like the Ritz-Carlton

The Ritz-Carlton, Toronto

Toronto, Canada

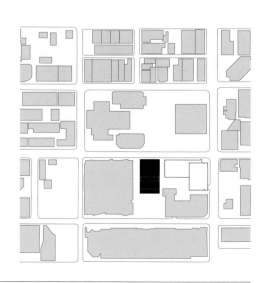

Location	Toronto, Canada
Year	2009
Address	181 Wellington Street West
	Toronto, Ontario M5V 3G7 Canada
Size	700,000 GSF / 65,000 GSM
Height	683 F / 208 M
Program	Hotel, serviced apartments, restaurant
Structure	Concrete and long span steel

One Jackson Square

New York, USA

Location	New York, USA
Year	2010
Address	122 Greenwich Avenue
	New York, New York 10011 USA
Size	65,000 GSF/ 6,000 GSM
Height	128 F / 39 M
Program	Residential, retail
Structure	Concrete

21 Davies Street

London, United Kingdom

Location	London, United Kingdom
Year	2004
Address	21 Davies Street
	London W1K 3DE United Kingdom
Size	61,440 GSF / 5,708 GSM
Program	Residential, office, retail
Structure	Concrete and steel

Canal Walk

Incheon, Korea

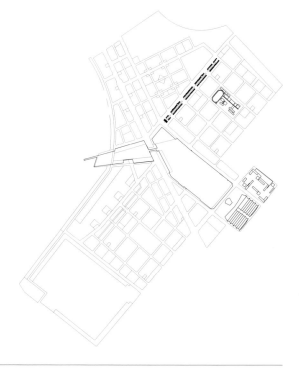

Location   Incheon, Korea
Year   2009
Address   23-1 Songdo-dong, Yeonsu-gu
           Incheon, Korea
Size   1,300,000 GSF / 120,000 GSM
Height   67 F / 20 M
Program   Office, retail, restaurant
Structure Concrete

First World Towers

Incheon, Korea

Location	Incheon, Korea
Year	2009
Address	4-1 Songdo-dong, Yeonsu-gu
	Incheon, Korea
Size	3,700,000 GSF / 344,000 GSM
Height	774 F / 236 M
Program	Residential, retail
Structure	Concrete

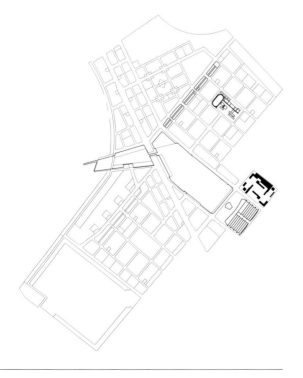

1ST WORLD
← 290 M

Transportation & Civic

Transportation & Civic

By Anthony Mosellie

Twelve years into the 21st Century, the world is struggling to emerge from the most severe economic downturn in a generation. As debt-saddled governments in the United States and Western Europe remain torn between stimulating growth and reducing deficits, crucial investment in infrastructure and other desperately needed government programs that would foster job growth has been deferred in the name of austerity. This growth/austerity dilemma is occurring at the precise moment that the West faces unprecedented competition from emerging Asian economic giants such as China. While the economic crisis appears to be subsiding, the political divide in America has all but extinguished hope for the same type of Depression-era governmental investment in public and civic works that laid the foundation for the country's prolonged growth in the decades that followed.

Facing decreasing tax revenues, increased deficit spending and the inability to raise capital through the traditionally low cost municipal bond markets, local and national governments have turned to the private sector to step in. The recent increase in Public Private Partnerships (PPP) projects provides governments with a much-needed conduit to address the lack of funds for public projects; however, privatization risks governmental abdication of the social responsibility associated with civic projects. It is imperative that the civic notion of building projects is for the greater good. This is where architects can play a vital role in the process, ensuring that design excellence and quality form the cornerstone of the public private partnership.

KPF's experience on civic projects has included both direct appointments by government entities and significant commissions through PPP's. On the US Airways International Terminal One project at the Philadelphia International Airport, the selection of US Airways as "developer" enabled the City of Philadelphia to design and construct the new $1 billion terminal in only four years. The decidedly private sector approach to construction procurement made the project attractive to the upper echelon of trade contractors that normally avoid public sector projects. The overall success of the project was due in great part to the alignment of aspirations between the City of Philadelphia and US Airways. KPF was fortunate to have been jointly selected by both parties and received a great deal of support during the entire process, enabling us to create a civic facility that is both architecturally significant and practical. Distinct from conventional air transport facilities which feature sunlit departure areas but afford deplaning passengers less than memorable amenities, arrival areas in the US Airways Terminal are given equal architectural significance. All arrival functions, including the baggage claim hall and sky-lit arrivals hall are located one floor above the departure hall. This inversion of the traditional sectional sequence between arrival and departure is fundamental to the terminal's conception as an international gateway, and gives travelers the experience of ascending through a light-filled route that increases in dramatic intensity.

For New Songdo City—a privately developed business district in Incheon, Korea—a suite of 'give-back' projects was conceived by the developer as a means of providing the sort of cultural infrastructure that would add significant economic value to the development as a whole while stimulating outside private investment. These projects include the Convensia convention center, the Chadwick International School, and Songdo Central Park—a 100-acre public park at the center of the New Songdo City master plan. As a civic landmark in the spirit of the great public works of the past, the park fulfills a wide variety of functions ranging from those associated with quality of life issues—access to nature, culture, education, and recreation—to those larger, more involved functions of city infrastructure such as storm water management, erosion control, and air quality assurance. Additionally, the park is the hub of a city-wide green space network that addresses pedestrian and bicycle circulation and transportation alternatives including an active water taxi that traverses the full length of the park via a half-mile long saltwater canal. As an early model of sustainability on a citywide scale, Songdo Central Park is a noteworthy example of Public Private Partnership demonstrating that green space adds value to new developments. In a world of increasingly dense cities, scarce resources, and multiple cultural perspectives, it is reassuring to see the degree to which the private sector has been compelled to embrace sustainable solutions.

At times, sustainable initiatives can be overrun by other mandates for civic projects. This is a common challenge in the post 9/11 era. The new U.S. Courthouse in Buffalo, New York, was on the drawing boards when the 2001 terrorist attacks struck America. Already delayed for quite some time due to the economic obstacles that challenged Western New York in the second half of the 20th century, the attacks and subsequent enhanced security requirements nearly derailed the project.

1. Daniel Patrick Moynihan U.S. Courthouse, New York, NY. Kohn Pedersen Fox, 1994. **2.** U.S. Courthouse, Minneapolis, MN. Kohn Pedersen Fox, 1997. **3.** Mark O. Hatfield U.S. Courthouse, Portland, OR. Kohn Pedersen Fox, 1997. **4.** U.S. Courthouse, Buffalo, NY. Kohn Pedersen Fox, 2011. **5.** Hoover Dam, Six Companies, Inc., 1936. **6.** Buffalo Niagara International Airport, Buffalo, NY. Kohn Pedersen Fox, 1997. **7.** Abu Dhabi International Airport Midfield Terminal Complex, Abu Dhabi, UAE. Kohn Pedersen Fox, 2017.

As the U.S. General Services Administration's (GSA) tenant and collaborating client, the Judges of the New York Western District were intent on addressing the public's role in the judicial process while participating in the great architectural legacy that is Buffalo and plans to renew its once vibrant downtown. In response, the scheme proposed that all of the primary public spaces be oriented towards Niagara Square— the heart of downtown as laid-out by Olmsted & Vaux and the location of Buffalo's historic City Hall. The architectural expression of these public spaces takes the form of two sweeping glass structures—the 10-story south wall that fronts the court floor lobbies, and the ceremonial entry pavilion featuring a silkscreened rendition of the Constitution across its glass walls. The transparency of these spaces serves as a metaphor for an open judicial process. Simultaneously, the views out of the public areas through the main glass wall were directly focused on Niagara Square in celebration of civic pride of Buffalo's heritage.

Despite the resounding approval of the concept by the Judges, the GSA, and civic leaders, security concerns challenged the most compelling elements of the design. By working in unison with judges and the GSA, we were able to ensure that the parti remained intact and all governmental mandates were successfully integrated into the building. Innovative strategies such as the positioning of the courthouse precisely on the site, the introduction of landscaped features to limit vehicular access, and the utilization of a glass veil on top of a predominantly solid wall ensured the sufficient hardening of the building. Without a doubt, a governmental client that was less committed to addressing civic obligation would

have abandoned the original design for a more conventional solution. Similarly, we were inspired by the judge's determination and persevered despite budgetary challenges.

Often investments in civic work run countercyclical to global economic trends. Historically, the very notion of increased public spending for governmental projects is in and of itself a civic and socially responsible response to difficult times. It remains to be seen, however, whether the more recent trend of public private partnerships will change the outcome from an architectural perspective. The major building initiatives borne out of the Great Depression such as the Hoover Dam not only improved the lives of many Americans by providing jobs and electrical power to rural sections of the country, but also came to be regarded as design and construction marvels. Depression-era projects like Rockefeller Center and the Chrysler building should serve as examples to today's developers. As designers, our responsibility is to passionately collaborate in this new generation of PPP civic works and to be a driving force in achieving high quality sustainable results.

Songdo Central Park

Incheon, Korea

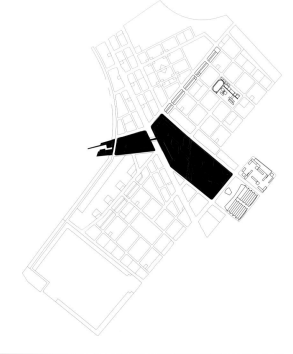

Location   Incheon, Korea
     Year   2009
Address   24-5, 31 Songdo-dong, Yeonsu-gu
          Incheon, Korea
     Size   100 Acres / 40 Hectares
Program   Recreation, culture, entertainment

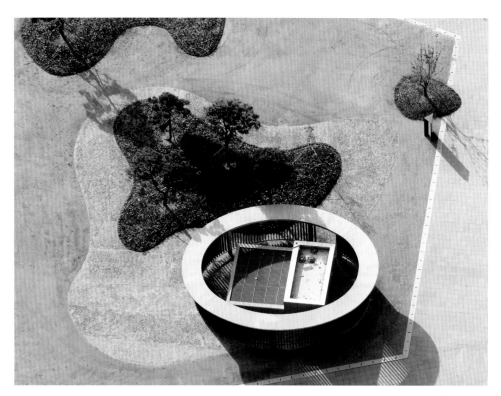

Songdo Convensia

Incheon, Korea

Location	Incheon, Korea
Year	2008
Address	6-1 Songdo-dong, Yeonsu-gu
	Incheon, Korea
Size	400,000 GSF / 37,000 GSM
Height	100 F / 30 M
Program	Convention, exhibition
Structure	Steel

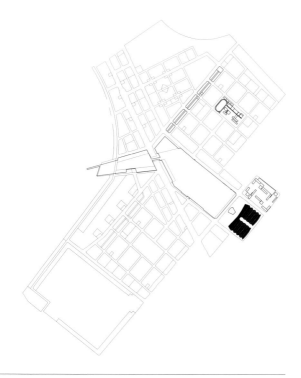

Ilsan Cultural Center

Kyongki-Do, Korea

Location	Kyongki-Do, Korea
Year	2007
Address	Ilsan-Ku
	Kyongki-Do, Korea
Size	522,750 GSF / 47,958 GSM
Height	118 F / 36 M
Program	Opera house, concert hall,
	library, cafeteria
Structure	Concrete and steel

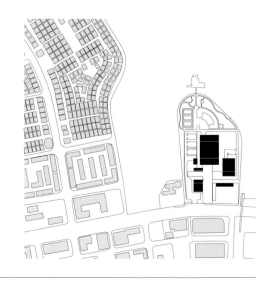

U.S. Courthouse

Buffalo, USA

Location	Buffalo, USA
Year	2011
Address	Niagara Square
	Buffalo, New York 14202 USA
Size	265,000 GSF / 25,000 GSM
Height	180 F / 55 M
Program	Courtrooms, chambers, U.S. marshall spaces,
	offices, below grade parking
Structure	Steel

Dulles International Airport AeroTrain C-Gates Station

Chantilly, USA

Location	Chantilly, USA
Year	2011
Address	3860 Centerview Drive
	Chantilly, Virginia 20001 USA
Size	234,215 GSF / 21,759 GSM
Program	Rail station, pedestrian connector tunnel, ancillary facilities
Structure	Steel

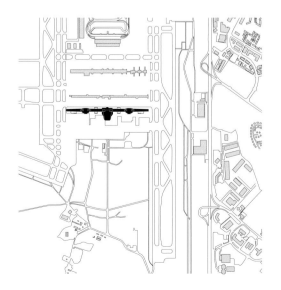

US Airways International Terminal One Philadelphia International Airport

Philadelphia, USA

Location	Philadelphia, USA
Year	2003
Address	8401 Executive Avenue
	Philadelphia, Pennsylvania 19153 USA
Size	780,000 GSF / 72,464 GSM
Program	Passenger terminal, airside and landside
	facilities, cargo and baggage handling,
	transit connection
Structure	Concrete and steel

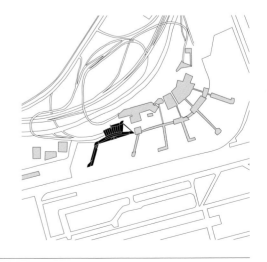

Mixed-Use

Mixed-Use

By Paul Katz

In a relatively short period, the mixed-use building has transformed our perception of urban life. Whether in a single structure or a composition of buildings (often towers), residential, office, cultural, hotel and retail amenities are increasingly linked together whereas not too long ago they were almost exclusively segregated into single-use facilities. This multi-program configuration, optimizing the use of land and public infrastructure, has begun to transform city centers in the post-industrial world, as well as rapidly emerging markets, and played a key role in the development of the "global city."

The global city—"a city that has a direct and tangible impact on global affairs through socioeconomic, cultural, and/or political means"— emerged in the 1980s as the result of widespread financial deregulation and technological advances that fueled the rise of service and knowledge-based economies, as well as transformation of the postwar political environment, epitomized by the fall of the Berlin Wall in 1991. The architecture that paralleled these changes demonstrated a new appreciation of urbanism, public space, and the end of the dogmatic form of Modernism and rigid urban zoning that had defined the cities of the postwar period.

At KPF during this era, we employed a variety of strategies such as "collage and contextualism" to design commercial and public buildings in North America based on the heritage and values of Western architecture. These approaches validated both the importance of the inner city core and the role of the large building—in particular the office tower—as its basic urban building block. We brought these ideas to our work in Europe, and then to Asia, through the portal of

Japan, whose economy and global companies were at their zenith. However, when we arrived in Japan we found that many of our assumptions and concepts that were rooted in Western architecture were questioned by the Japanese who wished to embrace their own traditions of urbanism and space while acceding to their dependence of technology. The Japanese synthesis of these forces was termed Metabolism, which was inspirational to us and a relevant alternative to the Postmodernism of the 1980s. At the same time we found common ground with our collaborators in their affinity for the craft of building and their focus on the quality of detail.

Working together with our Japanese colleagues and clients, we started thinking differently about scale and very large commercial projects with regard to both their internal organization as well as their integration in the cities in which they were embedded. The scale of these projects, often as large as three million square feet in a single building, was bigger and more audacious than we had ever seen. The design process required larger teams suited to the development of highly complex elements designed simultaneously over long periods of time and frequently adjusted for technical, budgetary and commercial reasons. The KPF culture, with its emphasis on collaboration rather than on the individual, suited the management of this kind of design effort, and was of great interest to our Japanese colleagues who themselves were so interested in the balance between teamwork and individual creativity.

This new approach was exemplified in our work creating both JR Central Towers and Station in Nagoya (1989–2000) and

Roppongi Hills in Tokyo (1991–2005) each of which involved tremendous scale, complexity and a continuous design effort that spanned over a decade. Our initial frames of reference, defined by our memory, culture and language, were at odds with these projects. However, over time we learned to think about the urban mixed-use project differently, ultimately preparing us for the complex needs of the 21st-century city.

Tokyo, the world's largest city, is in some ways a possible version of our own future and, at its center, Roppongi Hills, the most influential and visionary development. In designing the complex, we sought to reinvent the urban lifestyle. We reconsidered each of the functional typologies and placed greater importance on semi-public spaces and landscaped gardens, components previously overlooked in similar urban developments. In many regards, this mixed-use project represents micro-urbanism in the form of an "Ideal City" but purposely has no boundaries and seamlessly blends into the immediate context of much smaller buildings, which, as a consequence, has experienced incredible revitalization.

Roppongi Hills led directly to a second collaboration with the late Minoru Mori in Shanghai on the Shanghai World Financial Center, the tallest building in China, and an excellent example of the mixed-use building type realized in a single, vertical form or "vertical city." As with other mixed-use projects, the Shanghai World Financial Center is the result of our interaction with visionary individuals, patrons and companies who see the potential of a commercial development beyond financial profit as an opportunity—if not an obligation—to improve the lives of the city's inhabitants.

The Shanghai World Financial Center was completed in the midst of an unprecedented and still ongoing urban and economic boom in Asia, which has created the need for large multi-building projects and, at an ever greater scale, entirely new districts such as the expansion of Singapore's CBD with One Raffles Quay and the Marina Bay Financial Centre and the Songdo International Business District, which occupies over 1,500 acres of reclaimed land on the west coast of Incheon, Korea.

Meanwhile, in North America and Europe, we have come full circle, adopting many of the strategies we refined in Asia on projects such as Hudson Yards, leading the dramatic transformation of the far West Side, one of New York City's few undeveloped neighborhoods. Our goal, similar to the one we had for Roppongi Hills, is to reinvent the neighborhood while seamlessly blending with the surrounding context to create dynamic spaces and contribute to an improved urban lifestyle, a lifestyle that is part of a new "postindustrial" city in which increased density, mixed uses, public space, and the integration of public transportation create a dynamic never before experienced in the urban realm.

Roppongi Hills

Tokyo, Japan

Location	Tokyo, Japan
Year	2003
Address	Roppongi 6-Chome
	Minato-ku
	Tokyo 106-0032 Japan
Size	6,700,000 GSF / 622,000 GSM
Height	781 F / 238 M
Program	Office, retail, residential, hotel,
	public plaza, performing arts theatre,
	art museum, TV broadcast,
	transit connection
Structure	Concrete

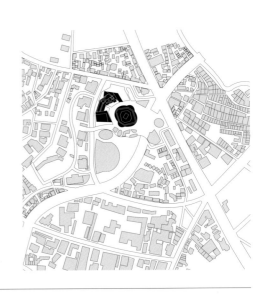

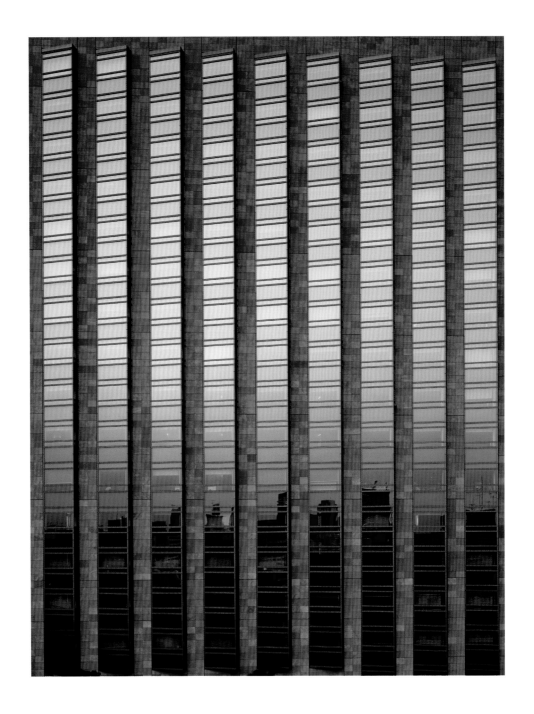

Espirito Santo Plaza

Miami, USA

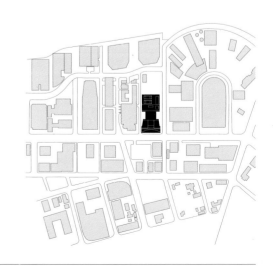

Location	Miami, USA
Year	2004
Address	1395 Brickell Avenue
	Miami, Florida 33131 USA
Size	1,200,000 GSF / 111,000 GSM
Height	483 F / 147 M
Program	Office, hotel, residential, parking
Structure	Concrete

One Central

Macau

Location Macau SAR
Year 2009
Address Avenida Dr Sun Yat Sen
Macau SAR
Size 2,300,000 GSF / 215,000 GSM
Height Tower: 558 F / 170 M
Program Hotel, residential, retail, parking
Structure Concrete

Palace 66

Shenyang, China

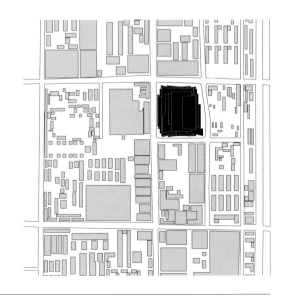

Location   Shenyang, China
Year   2010
Address   128 Zhongjie Lu
            Shenyang 100161 China
Size   1,200,000 GSF / 109,000 GSM
Height   79 F / 24 M
Program   Retail, entertainment
Structure   Concrete

China Central Place

Beijing, China

Location	Beijing, China
Year	2007
Address	6 Xi Da Wang Nan Lu Road
	Beijing 100022 China
Size	6,500,000 GSF / 619,461 GSM
Height	548 F / 167 M
Program	Office, hotel, residential, retail,
	public plazas
Structure	Concrete and steel

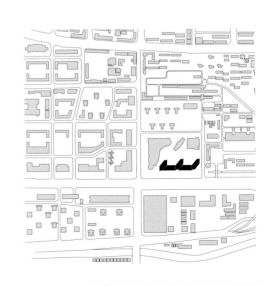

Northeast Asia Trade Tower

Incheon, Korea

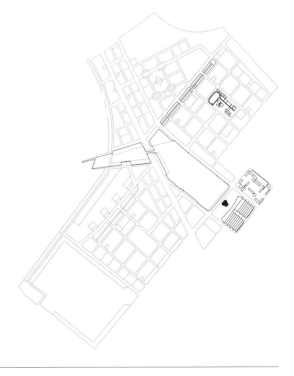

Location	Incheon, Korea
Year	2010
Address	Songdo-dong, Yeonsu-gu
	Incheon, Korea
Size	1,500,000 GSF / 139,000 GSM
Height	1,001 F / 305 M
Program	Office, residential, hotel, retail,
	observation deck, private club, parking
Structure	Concrete

One Raffles Quay & Marina Bay Financial Centre

Singapore

Location	Singapore
Year	One Raffles Quay: 2007
	Marina Bay Financial Centre: 2012
Address	Marina Boulevard
	Singapore 0397797
Size	One Raffles Quay:
	1,590,000 GSF / 148,000 GSM
	Marina Bay Financial Centre:
	4,000,000 GSF / 372,000 GSM
Height	One Raffles Quay:
	787 F / 240 M
	Marina Bay Financial Centre:
	1,125 F / 343 M
Program	Office, residential, retail, public plaza,
	transit connection
Structure	Steel and concrete

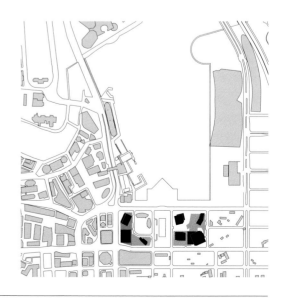

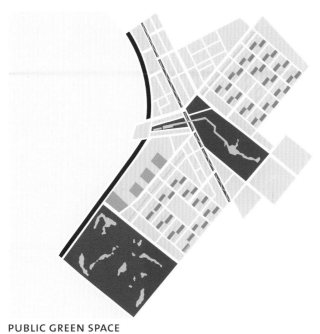

PUBLIC GREEN SPACE

PUBLIC TRANSPORTATION NETWORK

AIRPORT SHUTTLE BUS

• UTC BUS STOP

◦ SUBWAY STOP

—— BIKE PATH

- - - WATER TAXI

TRANSPORTATION CENTER

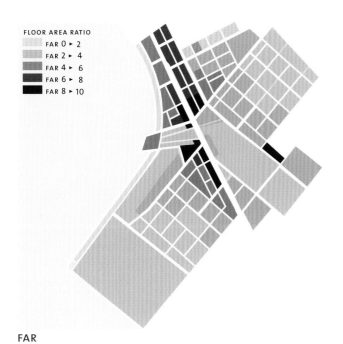

FLOOR AREA RATIO

FAR 0 ► 2

FAR 2 ► 4

FAR 4 ► 6

FAR 6 ► 8

FAR 8 ► 10

FAR

OFFICE MIXED-USED

RETAIL MIXED-USED

RESIDENTIAL MIXED-USE

RESIDENTIAL BLOCKS

SCHOOL PRIVATE

SCHOOL PUBLIC

HOTEL

HOSPITAL

CONVENTION CENTER

GOVERNMENT CENTER

CULTURE CENTER

DISTRIBUTION OF BUILDING TYPES

Meixi Lake

Changsha, China

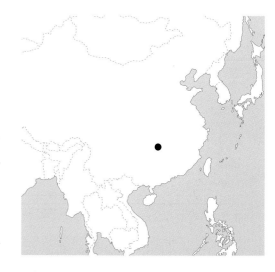

Location Changsha, China
Year 2010
Size 1,600 Acres / 647 Hectares

PUBLIC GREEN SPACE

- WATER
- PARK/PLAZA
- COURTYARD

PUBLIC TRANSPORTATION NETWORK

TO LANGFANG
TO LANGFANG
TO 2ND CAPITAL AIRPORT
TO LANGFANG

- ◄► AIRPORT RAIL AND STATION
- SUBWAY AND STATION
- LOCAL BUS AND STOP
- STREETCAR AND STOP

FAR

- FAR 0 ► 1.00
- FAR 1.01 ► 1.50
- FAR 1.51 ► 2.50
- FAR 2.51 ► 3.50
- FAR 3.51 ► 4.50

DISTRIBUTION OF BUILDING TYPES

- OFFICE / MIX-USED
- CONVENTION CENTER
- RESIDENTIAL
- EDUCATION
- RETAIL
- CULTURAL ISLAND
- MENUFACTURE

BSD City Master Plan

Tangerang, Indonesia

Location   Tangerang, Indonesia
Year   2030
Size   14,826 Acres / 6,000 Hectares

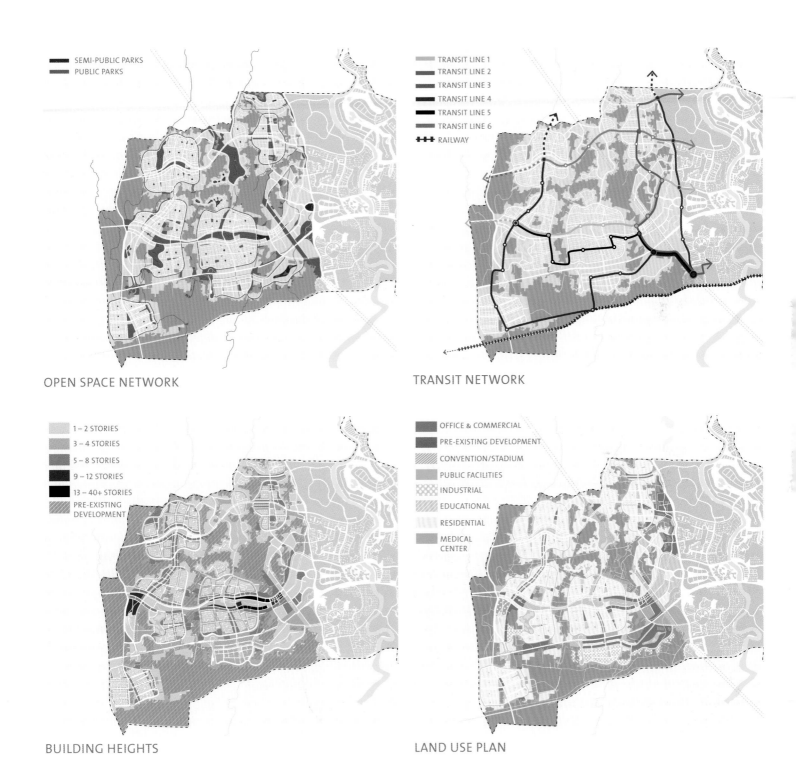

OPEN SPACE NETWORK

TRANSIT NETWORK

BUILDING HEIGHTS

LAND USE PLAN

Open Space Network legend:
- SEMI-PUBLIC PARKS
- PUBLIC PARKS

Transit Network legend:
- TRANSIT LINE 1
- TRANSIT LINE 2
- TRANSIT LINE 3
- TRANSIT LINE 4
- TRANSIT LINE 5
- TRANSIT LINE 6
- RAILWAY

Building Heights legend:
- 1 – 2 STORIES
- 3 – 4 STORIES
- 5 – 8 STORIES
- 9 – 12 STORIES
- 13 – 40+ STORIES
- PRE-EXISTING DEVELOPMENT

Land Use Plan legend:
- OFFICE & COMMERCIAL
- PRE-EXISTING DEVELOPMENT
- CONVENTION/STADIUM
- PUBLIC FACILITIES
- INDUSTRIAL
- EDUCATIONAL
- RESIDENTIAL
- MEDICAL CENTER

Postscript

The preceding chapters of this book depict buildings of various
scales and uses, in a broad range of geographies and site
conditions. There is, however, a common spirit that binds
this body of work together. In each project, the opportunity
underlying the immediate program issues has to do with
the relationship of architecture to the city. Even in the case
of sites that are removed from city centers, reference to the
larger urban construct provides a framework for the design.
Thus, airports are city gateways, and campuses can be seen as
abstracted models of urban form.

Ultimately, the success of these many KPF projects lies in the
way that they add to the energy of urban life. The images
of city skylines that appear in the following pages illustrate
this goal in its most literal sense: the impressive undulating
profiles of center city clusters are marked by bundled masses
of glass, metal and stone, distinct shapes of light and shadow.
Underlying this play of form are the operative functions
of closely coordinated uses, all supporting the efficiently
compacted patterns of modern life.

The intensity of these skylines, rising like graphs that record
the density of buildings and populations, is a mark of cultural
and commercial vitality. The early description of Manhattan
as the "island at the center of the earth" could apply not only
to New York, but also to each of these cities: London, Paris,
Hong Kong, Shanghai, Seoul, Singapore, and Tokyo. In each
case, the self-image of a metropolis as the center of commerce,
the font of ideas, the repository of history, and the breeding
ground of fashion, is reinforced by energetic structures that
strive to give new shape to these activities. These forms of
urban density, supported by new architectural solutions,
provide practical sustainable strategies for our contemporary
world. They also have the capacity to lift our spirits, and
inspire the imagination that feeds our culture.

Principals

Principals

A. Eugene Kohn, FAIA, RIBA, JIA
William Pedersen, FAIA, FAAR
William C. Louie, FAIA
Paul Katz, FAIA, HKIA
James von Klemperer, FAIA
Jill N. Lerner, FAIA
Michael Greene, AIA
Anthony Mosellie, AIA
Douglas Hocking, AIA, LEED AP BD+C
Robert C. Whitlock, AIA
Lloyd Sigal, AIA
John Bushell, ARB RIBA
Mustafa Chehabeddine
Dominic Dunn, AIA, LEED AP
Josh Chaiken, AIA
Brian Girard, AIA
Inkai Mu, AIA
Richard Nemeth, AIA
Trent Tesch, AIA
Shawn Duffy, AIA
Cristina Garcia, RIBA, COAC
Charles Ippolito, AIA, LEED AP BD+C
Hugh Trumbull, AIA

Directors

Forth Bagley
James Brogan, AIA
Bernard Chang, AIA, HKIA
Rebecca Cheng, RIBA, HKIA
Terri Cho
Brian Chung
Andrew Cleary, AIA, LEED AP
Ken Faulkner, ARB, RIBA
Bruce Fisher, AIA
Jens Hardvendel, MAA, ARB, RIBA
Hana Kassem, AIA, LEED AP
Jeffrey A. Kenoff, AIA
Marianne Kwok
Susan Lowance, AIA, LEED AP
Ko Makabe
David Malott
Shig Ogyu, AIA
Devin Ratliff, AIA, LEED AP
Paul Simovic, ARB, RIBA
Jerri Smith, LEED AP
Phillip White, AIA

Senior Associate Principals

Midori Ainoura
Chihiro Aoyama
Debra Asztalos, LEED AP
Rebecca Atkin, AIA, LEED AP
Brandon Buck
Luis E. Carmona, LEED AP
Theodore Carpinelli
Florence Chan, AIA, LEED AP
Linli Chen
Eunsook Choi, LEED AP
Shih-I Chou, AIA
Michael Cluff, AIA, LEED AP BD+C
David Cunningham, AIA
Claudia Cusumano, AIA, LEED AP
Hughy Dharmayoga
Yong Ding
Jean Dubuisson
Jim Dunster, ARB
Ahmed Elhusseiny
Anabel Fernandez, ARB, RIBA
Fernando Flores, LEED AP
Pedro Font-Alba, ARB
Ranieri Fontana-Giusti, ARB, RIBA
Elie Gamburg, AIA, LEED AP
Keisuke Hiei
Dennis Hill, ARB
Vivian Huang, AIA
Kazuki Katsuno
Chris Keeny, AIA
Heejin Kim, LEED AP
Min Kim, AIA
Laura King, AIA
Andrew Klare, Assosiate AIA
Sameer Kumar, AIA, LEED AP
Lei Li, LEED AP
Leif Lomo
Methanee Massirarat
John McIntyre, ANZIA
Jorge Mendoza, AIA
Jochen Menzer
Elaine Newman, AIA

Associate Principals

David Ottavio
Jinsuk Park
Russell Patterson
Gary Peters
Afshin Rafaat, LEED AP
Mark Rayson
Roger Robison, AIA
Lauren Schmidt, AIA, LEED AP
Luuc Schutte
William Schweber (Abu Dhabi)
Ana Sotrel
Gary Stluka, AIA
Mark Townsend
Gregory Waugh, AIA, LEED AP BD+C
Kevin Wegner
Albert S. Wei, LEED AP
Judy Wong, LEED AP
Nathan Wong, LEED AP
Tim Yu, ARB, RIBA
Zhizhe Yu, RAIA, LEED AP

Benjamin Albury
Paul Bae
Shiju Balakrishnan (Abu Dhabi)
Cobus Bothma
Britton Chambers
Ellen Chen, AIA, LEED AP
Yan Cheng
Li Min Ching, LEED AP
Audrey Choi
Matthew Chua
Hugo Corvalan
Daniel Dadoyan, AIA
Cherry Dai, LEED AP
Angela Davis
Tom Demetrion
Rebecca Egea, AIA, LEED AP
Hidehisa Furuta
Javier Galindo
Sammy Gao
Robert Graustein
Jonah Hansen
Sung woo Heo
Chia-Chen Hsieh
David Jaffe
Younhak Jeong, LEED AP
Kyu Hwan Jhin
Heejoon Jo
Alkis Klimathianos
Caroline Knoll
Devin Koelbl
Cindy Kubitz
Lee Ping Kwan, AIA, LEED AP
Joyce Lam, AIA
Edwin Lau, RAIC, LEED AP, Int'l Assoc. AIA
Yee Tak Lau, AIA, LEED AP, BEAM Pro
Hyunwoo Lee
Joon Hyuk Lee
Seunghyun Lee
Sam Li
Albert Lin
Yuan Lin, AIA

Rex Ma, LEED AP
Jennifer Martin
Greg Mell, AIA
Claudia Melniciuc
Michael Mitchell
Nyirabu Nyirabu
Maciej Olczyk, LEED AP
John Oliver, AIA
Charles Olsen, RIBA
Jennifer Pehr, AICP
Laura Piccardi, ARB
Karen Pui, ARB, RIBA, LEED AP
Dryden Razook
Pedro Reyna
David Riedel
Sean Roche
Heather Ross, AIA
Robert Scymanski
Ye Sheng
Don Shillingburg
Aleksandra Sojka
Bo Youn Song
Michiko Sumi
Ken Tan
Blanche Thomas-Tapper
Pamela Wackett
Mark Wang
Christopher White
Tae-Gyun Woo, AIA
Yi Xiong
Chen Yang
Najwan Yassin
Alanna Zie, ARB, RIBA

Selected Building Credits
2003–2012

Supertall

Shanghai World Financial Center
Shanghai, China
2008
Client: Mori Building Company. Design Principal: William Pedersen. Managing Principal: A. Eugene Kohn. Managing Principal: Paul Katz. Senior Designer: Joshua Chaiken. Senior Designer: Ko Makabe. Senior Designer: David Malott. Job Captain: Roger Robison. Project Team: Michael Bentley, Keisuke Hiei, James Jenkins, Kazuki Katsuno, Christopher Knotz, Kuinori Maeda, Americo Soza, Jonathan Wall, Shinichiro Yorita, Marisa Yu. Project Architect and Engineer: Mori Building Company. Local Design Institute: East China Architectural Design & Research Institute. Executive Architect: Irie Miyake Architects & Engineers. Architect of Record: Shanghai Modern Architecture Design Group. Contractor: China State Construction Engineering Corporation (CSCEC) and Shanghai Construction (Group) General Co. Structural Engineer: Leslie Robertson Associates R.L.L.P. M/E/P Engineer: Kenchiku Setsubi Sekkei Kenkyusho. Curtain Wall Engineer: ALT Cladding & Design, Inc. Geotechnical: Shannon & Wilson. Landscape Designer: Mori Building Company. Lighting Design: Motoko Ishii Lighting Design. Fire Safety: Rolf Jensen & Associates. Wind Engineer: Alan Davenport Wind Engineering Group. Façade Maintenance: Nihon Bisoh Co, Ltd.

International Commerce Center
Hong Kong, SAR
2011
Client: Harbour Vantage Management Limited / Sun Hung Kai Properties. Design Principal: William Pedersen. Managing Principal: Paul Katz. Senior Designer: Kar-Hwa Ho. Senior Designer: Eric Howeler. Senior Designer: David Malott. Senior Designer: Trent Tesch. Project Manager: Shawn Duffy. Project Manager: Andreas Hausler. Job Captain: Glen DaCosta. Project Team: Michael Arad, Bruno Caballe-Munill, Yook Chan, Yaminay Chaudhri, Peter Epstein, Clarisa Garcia-Fresco, Ignacio Iratchet, John Lucas, Eric Mark, Gene Miao, Yin Wai Teh, Ernesto Trindade, Jedidiah Weeks, Marisa Yiu, Sergy Yushchenko, Tadyuki Zetsu. Associate Architect: Wong & Ouyang (HK) Ltd. Structural and Civil Engineer: Arup. M/E/P Engineer: JRPL. Exterior Wall: ALT Cladding & Design, Inc. Fire Safety Engineer: Arup Fire (HK). Vertical Transportation: Lerch Bates & Associates, Inc. Landscape Architect: Belt Collins & Associates. Quantity Surveyors: WTP.

Corporate Headquarters

Samsung Seocho Headquarters
Seoul, Korea
2008
Client: Samsung Corporation. Design Principal: William Pedersen. Design Principal: Peter Schubert. Managing Principal: Michael Greene. Managing Principal: A. Eugene Kohn. Senior Designer: Thomas Schlesser. Senior Designer: Trent Tesch. Project Manager: Lloyd Sigal. Project Team: Kate Bowman, Eunsook Choi, Luigi Ciaccia, Adam Felchner, Bruce Fisher, Pedro Font-Alba, Chia-Chien Hsieh, Ryan Hullinger, Charles Lamy, Joon-Hyuk Lee, Shin Nishigaki, Daniel Shaddick. Architect of Record: SAMOO. Structural Engineer of Record: Chung-Lim Structural Consultant. Structural Engineer: Arup. M/E/P Engineer: Syska & Hennessy. Civil Engineer: Saegil Engineering & Consulting. Mechanical Engineering Consultant: Sun Jin Engineers Consultant Company. Curtain Wall: ALT Cladding & Design, Inc. Landscape Architect: Peter Walker & Partners. Lighting Design: Tillotson Design Associates. Vertical Transportation: Van Deusen & Associates. Cost Estimate: Hanscomb Faithful & Gould, Inc. Construction Manager: Samsung Construction Company.

Endesa Headquarters
Madrid, Spain
2003
Client: Grupo ENDESA SA. Senior Designer: Cristina Garcia. Project Manager; James Outen. Project Team: Yanko Apostolov, Jean Cedric de Foy, Geoff Cartwright, Chris Challonner, Susana de la Rosa, Cosmo De Piro, John Gordon, Simon Hall, Tony Lett, Paul Lynch, Neil Merryweather, Graham Newell, Ross Page, Fernando Palacios, Robert Peebles, Lee Polisano, Eliseo Rabbi, Jorge Seabrooke, Simon Stubbs, Neus Viu, Andrew Watts, Dean Weeden, Alex Yule. Associate Architect: Rafael de La-Hoz Arquitectos S.L. M/E/P Consultant: Battle McCarthy. Engineering: Prointec, Pondio Ingenieros, Rafael Urculo. Roof Steel Structure: Horta. Structural Glass Engineer: Bellapart Engineering. Curtain Wall Cladding/Skylights: Permasteelisa España S.A. Vertical Transportation: Thyssen Boetticher. Security: Indra Sistemas de Seguridad. Project Management: Gerens Hill International S.A. Quality Surveyors: Davis Langdon & Everest. Quality Control: Buro Veritas Español.

RBC Centre
Toronto, Canada
2009
Client: The Cadillac Fairview Corporation Limited. Managing Principal: Paul Katz. Senior Designer: Joshua Chaiken. Project Manager: Gregory Waugh. Project Team: Kesler Flores, Terry Hudak, David Jaffe, Kazuki Katsuno, Lee Ping

Kwan, Keon-Soo Nam, Ana Sotrel. Architect of Record: Bregman+Hamann. Collaborating Design Architect: Sweeny Sterling Finlayson & Co. Architects Inc. Contractor: PCL Construction. Structural Engineer: Yolles Partnership. Mechanical Engineer: The Mitchell Partnership Inc. Electrical Engineer: Mulvey + Banani. Landscape Architect: Strybos & Associates. Environmental Specialist: Enermodal Engineering. Traffic Consultant: BA Consulting Group, Ltd.

Mirae Asset Tower
Shanghai, China
2009
Client: Mirae Asset MAPS Investment Management Co., Ltd., Shanghai Min Tai Real Estate Co. Ltd. Design Principal: James von Klemperer. Managing Principal: Inkai Mu. Senior Designer: Jason Zerafa. Project Manager: Scott Springer. Job Captain: Vivian Huang. Project Team: Luis E. Carmona, Rebecca Cheng, Thomas Coldefy, Luis de la Fuente, David Goldschmidt, Markus Hoecherl, Beatriz Marin, Shin Nishigaki, Manon Pare, Jose Sanchez, Chris Zhang, Xiaolu Zhou. Local Architect: East China Architectural Design & Research Institute Co. Ltd. Structural, M&E and Curtain Wall Engineer: Arup.

China Huaneng Group Headquarters
Beijing, China
2010
Client: China Huaneng Group. Design Principal: William C. Louie. Managing Principal: Robert L. Cioppa. Senior Designer: Lei Li. Project Manager: Peter Gross. Project Manager: Inkai Mu. Job Captain: Angela Davis. Job Captain: Liping Gong. Project Team: Antonio Aros, Po-Ku Chen, Francis Edelman, Dean Ficek, Sam Huang, Roland K.S. Kang, Connie Lee, Sam K.S. Leung, Hao Li, Josh Lo, Jennifer Martin, Douglas Wu, Competition Team: Eunsook Choi, Jochen Menzer, Hugh Trumbull, Xiaofeng Zhu. Associate Architect: East China Architectural Design & Research Institute Co., Ltd. Structural and M/E/P Engineer: East China Architectural design & Research Institute Co., Ltd. Curtain Wall: ALT Cladding & Design, Inc. Skylight Structure: Arup. Lighting Design: Bradston Partnership. Terracotta Panel Glazing Design: Christine Jetten. Façade Maintenance: Entek Engineering. Fountain System Design: HOBBS Architectural Fountains.

CNOOC Headquarters
Beijing, China
2006
Client: China National Offshore Oil Corporation (CNOOC). Design Principal: William C. Louie. Senior Designer: Hugh Trumbull. Project Manager: Peter Gross. Job Captain: Jae

Hyun Chang. Project Team: Knute Haglund, Daniel Killinger, Jennifer Martin, Carlos Rodriguez, Eva Tiedemann, Xiaofeng Zhu. Associate Architect, Local Design Institute: China Architecture Design & Research Group. Contractor: CSCEC, CNYD (Podium), Gartner Hong Kong (Tower). Landscape Design: Beijing Botanical Gardens, Jinghua Landscape. Lighting: Branston Partnership. Exterior Lighting: China Academy of Building Research. Exterior Wall and Building Maintenance: Meinhardt Façade Technologies. Ceramicist: Christine Jetten.

Posteel Tower
Seoul, Korea
2002
Client: POSCO. Design Principal: William Pedersen. Design Principal: Peter Schubert. Senior Designer: Kar-Haw Ho. Project Manager: Chulhong Min. Job Captain: Glen DaCosta. Project Team: Bernardo Gogna, Andrew Kawahara, Dohee Lee, Susana Su. Associate Architect: Pos-A. C. Co., Ltd. Structural Engineer: Arup. Service Engineer: Arup. Main Contractor: POSEC.

Abu Dhabi Investment Authority Headquarters
Abu Dhabi, United Arab Emirates
2007
Client: Abu Dhabi Investment Authority (ADIA). Design Principal: David Leventhal. Senior Designer: Kevin Flanagan. Project Manager: Kieran Breen. Job Captain: David Doody. Project Team: James Amos, Jacqueline Bignell, Ute Burkhardt-Heinlein, Pedro Font-Alba, Lee Marsden, Paul Simovic, Blair Stewart, Andreas Trisveis. Mechanical and Electrical Engineer: Buro Happold Limited. Contractor: Samsung Engineering & Construction Company, Ltd. Program Manager: CRSS International Inc. Interior Designer: Gensler. Landscape Architect: EDAW Ltd. (UK). Cost Consultant: Hanscomb, Inc. Security: Schiff & Associates, Inc. Vertical Transportation: John A. Van Deusen & Associates, Inc. Lighting: Isometrix Lighting & Design. Audio Visual: Shen Milsom & Wilke, Inc.

Clifford Chance Headquarters
London, United Kingdom
2002
Client: Canary Wharf Limited. Managing Principal: Paul Katz. Senior Designer: Marianne Kwok. Senior Designer: Kar-Hwa Ho. Senior Designer: Duncan Reid. Project Manager: Richard Nemeth. Project Team: Marcus Acheson, Gertrudis Brens, Li-Min Ching, Sebastian Cifuentes, Jamil Coppin, Parker Eberhard, Peter Epstein, Mark Gausepohl, Jaskran Kalirai, Yvonne Lam, Bonnie Leung, Juan Francisco Lladser, David Malott, Gaetane Michaux, Hisanori Mitsui,

Edward Robinson. Associate Architect: Adamson Associates Architects. Interior Architect: Gensler. Structural Engineer: Yolles Partnership Inc. M/E/P Engineer: HH Angus & Associates Ltd. Contractor: Canary Wharf Contractors. Curtain Wall Trade Contractor: Scheldebouw B.V. Façade Maintenance: Reef Associates Ltd. Lighting: Isometrix Lighting & Design. North Canopy Engineer: Dewhurst MacFarlane and Partners. Security: Hatch Mott MacDonald.

Stephen M. Ross School of Business, University of Michigan
Ann Arbor, USA
2009
Client: University of Michigan. Design Principal: William Pedersen. Managing Principal: Jill N. Lerner. Senior Designer: Jerri Smith. Project Manager: Charles Ippolito. Lead Programmer/Planner: Susan Lowance. Job Captain: Phillip White. Interiors Job Captain: David Ottavio. Project Team: Collin Anderson, Robert L. Cioppa, Katherine Corsico, Angela Duncan-Davis, Jacquelyn Fung, Robert Graustein, Adolfo Guerrero, Lauren Hibner, Younhak Jeong, Chris Keeny, Sooran Kim, Andrew Klare, Kenichi Noguchi, Tae-Gyun Woo. Structural Engineer: TTG. M/E/P and F/P Engineer: Cosentini Associates. Façade Consulting: Heitmann & Associates Inc. Landscape: JJR. Audio Visual: Shen Milsom & Wilke.

Science Teaching and Student Services Center, University of Minnesota
Minneapolis, USA
2010
Client: University of Minnesota. Design Principal: William Pedersen. Managing Principal: Robert L. Cioppa. Managing Principal: Michael Greene. Senior Designer: Andrew Klare. Senior Designer: Jerri Smith. Project Manager: Phillip White. Environmental Systems: Tiffany Broyles. Project Team: Paul Bae, Britton Chambers, Michael Cluff, Jeremiah Geiman, Terry Hudak, Ephraim Lasar, Gregory Mell, Tae-Gyun Woo. Executive Architect: Hammel, Green and Abrahamson, Inc. Structural, Civil and M/E/P Engineer, Landscape Architect, Lighting Design: Hammel, Green and Abrahamson, Inc. Construction Manager: McGough Construction Company, Inc. Exterior Wall Consultant: Bill Young / Axis Group. Vertical Transportation: Lerch Bates & Associates, Inc. Energy Consultant: The Weidt Group. Acoustic/Audio Visual: Shen Milsom & Wilke.

Alvah H. Chapman Jr. Graduate School of Business, Florida International University
Miami, USA
2007
Client: Florida International University. Design Principal: William Pedersen. Managing Principal: Jill N. Lerner. Senior Designer: Hana Kassem. Project Manager: Susan Lowance. Project Team: Anne-Marie Armstrong, Andreas Buettner, Rachel Eck, Roger Goodhill, Bruce Hancock, James Jenkins, Florena Nemteanu, David Ottavio, Becky Patterson, Devin Ratliff, Poonam Sharma, Elana Tenebaum. Associate Architect: BEA International. Structural and Civil Engineer: BEA International. M/E/P Engineer: TLC Engineering.

Landscape: Laura Llerena & Associates. Acoustic: Harvey Marshall Berling Associates.

Prince's Gardens Redevelopment, Imperial College
London, United Kingdom
2009
Client: Imperial College. Design Principal: Fred Pilbrow. Managing Principal: David Leventhal. Project Manager: Jon Neville-Jones. Project Team: Sara Aronsson, Simon Close, Matthew Crawford, Adelaide Degezelle, Rebecca Egea, Anabel Fernandez, Alice Fung, Jennifer Henry, Chris Hoevels, Andrea Jung, Jon Neville-Jones, Julie Norton, Bernard Storch, Eva Tiedemann, Timothy Yu. Engineering: London Engineering Company. Mechanical and Electrical Engineer: Atelier Ten. Structural Engineer: Adams Kara Taylor. Construction Manager: Bovis Lend Lease (UK). Project Management: Arup. Planning Consultants: Gerald Eve. Archaeology: The Museum of London Archeology Service. Acoustic: Acoustic Design Ltd. Lighting: Isometrix Lighting & Design. Lighting: Sentinel. Vertical Transportation: Lerch Bates.

Chadwick International School
Incheon, Korea
2010
Client: Gale International and Posco E&C. Design Principal: James von Klemperer. Managing Principal: Gregory Clement. Senior Designer: Methanee Massirarat. Project Manager: Gregory Weithmam. Job Captain: Ming Leung. Job Captain (On Site): Daniel Treinen. Project Team: Chihiro Aoyama, Allison Austin, Jason Carney, David Goldschmidt, Aaron Kominos-Smith, Jinseuk Lee, Joon-Hyuk Lee, Kangsoo Lee, Irene Molina, Marc Remshardt, Eric Smith, Xiaolu Zhou. Associate Architect: Gansam Partners. M/E/P Engineer & Lighting: Cosentini. Consulting Engineers: Arup. Contractor: POSCO E&C. Curtain Wall: CDC. Façade Maintenance: Entek. Acoustical: Cerami. Educational Planner: Ray Bordwell.

INCS Zero Factory
Nagano, Japan
2008
Client: INCS, Inc. Design Principal: William Pedersen. Managing Principal: Paul Katz. Senior Designer: Ko Makabe. Project Team: Akihide Hanamura, Christopher Knotz. Structural, Mechanical, Electrical Engineer and Contractor: Maeda Corporation. Lighting Design: Yamada Shomei Lighting Co., Ltd.

Office Buildings

Heron Tower
London, United Kingdom
2011
Client: Heron Corporation International. Design Principal: Fred Pilbrow. Managing Principal: Lee Polisano. Senior Designer: Paul Simovic. Job Captain: Dennis Hill. Project Team: Marcos Blanes, Samantha Cooke, Elzbieta Dabkowska, Kei-Lu Dinsdale, Ivan Equihua, Keb Garavito, Turgay Hakverdi, Matt Jackson, Takatomo Kashiwabara, Puneet Khanna, Hannah Ko, Leif Lomo, Iaia Loppi, Claudia Maggi, Clare Mason, Raita Nakajima, Ross Page, Robert Peebles, Laura Piccardi, Milica Plinston, Rosa Rius, Shibboleth Shecter, Marcus Springer, Alexander Stewart, Danielle Tinero, Tim Yu. Structural Engineer: Arup. Main Contractor: Skanska. Project Manager: Mace. Building Services: Foreman Roberts. Planning Consultant: DP9. Landscape: Charles Funke.

505 Fifth Avenue
New York, USA
2005
Client: Kipp-Stawski Management Group. Design Principal: Douglas Hocking. Managing Principal: Paul Katz. Project Manager: Christopher Stoddard. Project Team: Theodore Carpinelli, Li-Min Ching, Miranti Gumayana, Wendy Hanes, John Lucas, Lloyd Sigal. Structural Engineer: Rosenwasser & Grossman. M/E/P Engineer: Jaros Baum & Bolles Consulting Engineers. Civil Engineer: Langan. Construction Manager: Pavarini McGovern. Curtain Wall: Benson Industries LLC. Exterior Wall: Gordon H. Smith Corporation. Code Consultant: Metropolis. Specifications: Construction Specifications, Inc. Lighting: Isometrix Lighting & Design, S+S Design. Vertical Transportation: Van Deusen & Associates. Zoning: Development Consulting Services.

555 Mission Street
San Francisco, USA
2009
Client: TST Mission Street LLC and Tishman Speyer. Design Principal: Douglas Hocking. Managing Principal: A. Eugene Kohn. Managing Principal: Anthony Mosellie. Senior Designer: Li-Min Ching. Project Manager: Robert Hartwig. Project Team: Liatt Avigdor, Jonathan Chace, Hanna Chang, Pedro Font-Alba, Laura Foxman, Anders Hausler, David Jaffe, Sera Kimura, SooHee Lee, David Lukes, Angie Michail, Thomas Schlesser, Peter Schubert, David Tasman, Helen Wang, Cheung Wong. Collaborating Architect: Heller Manus Architects. M/E/P Engineer: Flack & Kurtz Consulting Engineers. Civil Engineer: BKF Engineers. Contractor: Turner Construction Company. Curtain Wall: Curtain Wall Design & Consulting, Inc. Curtain Wall Contractor: Benson

Industries, LLC. Code and Life Safety Consultant: Rolf Jensen & Associates, Inc. Specifications: Topflight Specs. Geotechnical: Treadwell & Rollo. Exterior Maintenance: Citadel Consulting, Inc. Lighting Design: Horton Lees Brogden. Vertical Transportation: Edgett Williams Consulting Group, Inc. Acoustics: Shen Milsom & Wilke, Inc. Green Building Consultants: Simon and Associates. Permit Consultant: Jaidin Consuting Group. Parking: Walker Parking Consultants. Waterproofing: Simpson Gumpertz & Heger, Inc. Graphic Design: Kate Keating Associates. Landscape Architect: Hargreaves Associates.

Infinity Tower
São Paulo, Brazil
2012
Client: YUNY Incorporadora / GTIS Partners. Design Principal: William C. Louie. Managing Principal: A. Eugene Kohn. Senior Designer: Jochen Menzer. Project Manager: Andrew Cleary. Project Manager: Dominic Dunn. Project Team: Debra Asztalos, Hernaldo Flores, Arthur Tseng, Rachel Villata. Local Architect: Aflalo & Gasperini Arquitetos. Structural Engineer: Aluizio A. M. D'Avila. Mechanical Engineer: Teknika. Exterior Wall Consultant: Israel Berger & Associates, LLC. Landscape Architect: D/W Santana. LEED Consultant: CTE.

Nihonbashi 1-Chome
Tokyo, Japan
2004
Client: Mitsui Fudosan Corporation, Tokyu Corporation, Tokyu Land Corporation. Design Principal: William Pedersen. Managing Principal: Paul Katz. Senior Designer: Tomas Alverez. Senior Designer: Ko Makabe. Project Manager: Andreas Hausler. Job Captain: Ernesto Trindade. Project Team: Li-Min Ching, Luis Fernandez, Lourdes Gavilanes, Ka-Kuen Lai, John Lucas, Allison McKenzie, Shinichiro Yorita. Architect of Record: Nihon Sekkei. Mechanical, Electrical, Structural Engineer: Nihon Sekkei. Contractor: Shimizu Mitsui Tokyo Joint Venture. Curtain Wall: ALT Cladding & Design, Inc. Lighting: ALG.

Wheelock Square
Shanghai, China
2010
Client: The Wharf (Holdings) Ltd. Design Principal: Robert Whitlock. Design Principal: William C. Louie. Senior Designer: Bruce Fisher. Project Team: Julian Goldman, Charles Ippolito, Wee Shen Khoo, Warren Kim, Jeremy Linzee, Sheng Lin, Dominico Lio, Roland K.S. Kang, Jeffery McKean, Richard Nugent, James Park, James Pfeiffer, James Suh, Marcela Villarroel, Judy Wong, Chris Zhang, Xiaofeng

Zhu. Associate Architect: Leigh & Orange. Structural Engineer: Arup and Maunsell Structural Consultants Ltd. M/E/P and Vertical Transportation: Parsons Brinckerhoff. Main Contractor: CSCEC. Curtain Wall: ALT Cladding. Curtain Wall Contractor: Gartner. Lighting: BPD. Landscape: Kenneth Ng & Associates. Graphics: Graphia.

Plaza 66
Shanghai, China
2006
Client: Hang Lung Properties Ltd. Design Principal: James von Klemperer. Managing Principal: Paul Katz. Senior Designer: Methanee Massirarat. Project Manager: Dominic Dunn. Job Captain: Shawn Duffy. Project Team: Andrew Berger, Lojung Huang, Diarmuid Kelly, Matthew Krissel, Andy Tsao, Phillip White, Nathan Wong. Local Design Institute: East China Architectural Design & Research Institute (ECADI). Structural Engineer: Thornton Tomasetti. M/E/P Engineer: Associated Construction Consultants. Wind Tunnel Engineering Construction: Rowan Williams Davies & Irwin, Inc. Vertical Transportation: Lerch Bates. QA/QC: Davis Langdon & Seah.

CSCEC Headquarters
Shanghai, China
2008
Client: China State Construction & Engineering Corporation. Design Principal: Robert Whitlock. Managing Principal: Paul Katz. Job Captain: Christopher Chan. Project Team: Shiju Balakrishnan, Rebecca Chan, Ami Dhruva, Fernando Flores, Manman Huang, Aman Krishan, Kyle Steinfeld, Hemmer Xu. Associate Architect: China State Construction International Design Institute. Structural Engineer: AECOM Maunsell. Mechanical Engineer: Meinhardt (Shanghai) Ltd. Main Contractor: CSCEC. Interior Contractor: XinLi. Curtain Wall Consultant: ALT Cladding. Curtain Wall Contractor: Yuanda. Lighting Design: Brandston Partnership Inc.

Repositioning

Unilever London Headquarters
London, United Kingdom
2007
Client: Unilever Plc. Senior Designer: John Bushell. Senior Designer, Interiors: Robert Hartwig. Project Team: Jeffery Ang, Jacqueline Bignell, Peck-San Chan, Simon Close, Clara Doty, Jim Dunster, Eva Esteban, Etain Fitzpatrick, Greg Hughes, Mark Hutchison, Andrew Jung, Takatomo Kashiwabara, Lydia Kim, Laura King, Paul Knight, Myung Lee, Wai Sem Lee, Cindy Liu, Laurey Lucree, Andrew McConachie, Daniel Moore, Raita Nakajima, Adrian Pang, Robert Peebles, Lee Polisano, Jorge Seabrook, Simon Stubbs, Stepan Toman, Ian Walker, Ryan Yiu, Timothy Yu, Alanna Zie. Structural and Services Engineer: Arup. Construction Manager: Bovis Lend Lease. Cost Consultant: Davis Langdon Mott Green Wall.

Tour First
Paris, France
2011
Client: AXA Rheims, Beacon Capital, Altarea Cogedim. Design Principal: Karen Cook. Managing Principal: A. Eugene Kohn. Senior Designer: Nicki Farantouri. Senior Designer: Cosmo De Piro. Senior Designer: Mustafa Chehabeddine. Senior Designer: Karl Sharro. Project Manager: Ranieri Fontana-Giusti. Project Manager (Finishes Package): Yrieix Martineau. Project Manager: David Doody. Project Manager: François Clement. Project Team: Yumeng Chan, Efrat Cohen, Alessandra Da Fieno, Kunal Dhavale, Gavin Eldred, Valerie Francou, Carmen Lau, Geraldine Lubert, Alessandra Luzzato, Jan Mackie, Christian Maro, Andrei Martin, Joelle Mansour, Dan Moore, Laura Petruso, Grace Tan, Sophia Tseliou, Ute Ubmheilein, Miglena Uzuncheva. Associate Architect: Saubot-Rouit Architectes. Structural and M/E/P Engineer: IOSIS. General Contractor: Bouygues Batiment Ile-De-France- Rénovation Privée. Site Project Management: Coteba. Façade Contractor: Belgo Metal N.V. Façade Contractor: Permasteelisa. Façade Contractor: RFR Partnership. Geotechnical: FUGRO. BMU Consultant: Reef Associated, Ltd. Sustainability Consultant: IOSIS. Sustainability Auditors: Le Sommer Environment. Finishes Package: BDM Architectures. Building Control: Socotec.

Centra Metropark
Iselin, USA
2011
Client: The Hampshire Companies. Managing Principal: A. Eugene Kohn. Managing Principal: Lloyd Sigal. Senior Designer: Hugh Trumbull. Project Manager: Devin Ratliff. Project Team: Alex Adarichev, Sam Leung, Gregory Mell, Allison Weinstein. Structural Engineer: DeSimone Consulting Engineers. M/E/P and FP Engineer: AMA Consulting Engineers. Contractor: Tishman Construction. Landscape Architect: Towers Golde. Lighting Design: S+S Lighting Design.

640 Fifth Avenue
New York, USA
2004
Client: Vornado Realty Trust. Design Principal: James von Klemperer. Managing Principal: A. Eugene Kohn. Senior Designer: Jason Zerafa. Senior Designer: Hughy Dharmayoga. Project Manager: Gregory Waugh. Job Captain: Charles Lamy. Job Captain (CA): Theodore Carpinelli. Project Team: Luis E. Carmona, Anna Crittenden, Adam Felchner, Clarisa Garcia-Fresco, Pablo Kawles, Warren Kim, Joanna Kuo, Manon Pare, Dylan Sauer, Eva Tiedemann, Michael Tunkey, Adam Woltag. Structural Engineer: Thornton Tomasetti. M/E/P Engineer: Goldman Copeland Associates, PC. Pre-Construction Consultant-Contractor: Pavarini Construction Co. Inc. Code Consultant: Jerome Gillman Consulting Architect, PC. Exterior Wall: Heitmann & Associates, Inc. Exterior Wall Maintenance: Entek Engineering, LLP. Vertical Transportation: Jenkins & Huntington, Inc. Zoning Consultant: Development Consulting Services, Inc.

The Landmark
Hong Kong, SAR
2007
Client: Hongkong Land Limited and Mandarin Oriental Hotel Group. Managing Principal: Paul Katz. Senior Designer: Kar-Hwa Ho. Project Manager: Shawn Duffy. Job Captain: Nathan Wong. Project Team: Darlington Brown, Sophia Chan, Li-Min Ching, Adelaide Degezelle, Peter Epstein, Pedro Font-Alba, Wendy Hanes, Keisuke Hiei, Chia-Chien Hsieh, Marianne Kwok, Bonnie Leung, Marisa Yiu, Sergey Yushenko. Architect of Record (Phase II): Aedas. Mechanical Engineer: Meinhardt. Electrical Engineer: Meinhardt. Structural Engineer: Maunsell Consultants Asia, Ltd. Curtain Wall: ALT Cladding. Fire Consultant: Arup. Lighting: Fisher Marantz Stone. Quality Surveyor: WT Partnership Ltd.

World Trade Center
Amsterdam, Netherlands
2004
Client: ING Vastgoed and Kantoren Foods Nederland Management. Managing Principal: Lee Polisano. Senior Designer: Ian Milne. Project Manager: Bernard Tulkens. Project Manager: Andre Van Oudhuesden. Job Captain: Dirk Vroegindeweij. Project Team: Jacqueline Daniels, Neil Merryweather, Ross Page, Cosmo de Piro, Mark Richard, Ramiro Salceda, Amy Schmieding, Chris Schnoover,

Dean Weeden. Associate Architect: Van den Oever, Zaaijer, Roodbeen & Partners. Structural Engineer: RFR Partnership. M/E/P Engineer: Ketel Raadgevende Ingenieurs. M/E/P Engineer: Royal Haskoning. Landscape: Ruwan Aluvihare.

Children's Hospital of Philadelphia
Philadelphia, USA
2006
Client: Children's Hospital of Philadelphia. Managing Principal: A. Eugene Kohn. Managing Principal: Jill N. Lerner. Design Principal: Peter Schubert. Senior Designer: Jerri Smith. Senior Technical Coordinator: Russell Patterson. Project Manager: Gregory Waugh. Project Manager (Phase III): Charles Ippolito. Job Captain: Andrew Cleary. Project Team: Vladimir Balla, Scott Baumberger, Carl Chapman, Lily Chiu, Kenneth Darbeau, Adam Felchner, Brian Girard, Miranti Gumayana, Ryan Hullinger, Eun Kim, Sean O'Brien, Cynthia Toyota, Nancy Yin. Associate Architect, Interiors, Phase I: Karlsberger. Architect of Record, Phase II: Robert D. Lynn Associates. Architect of Record, Phase III, Ballinger. Structural Engineer: Cagley Harman & Associates. Structural Engineer, Phase III: Arup. Mechanical Engineer: Bard, Rao + Athanas Consulting Engineers, Inc. Civil Engineer: Pennoni Associates, Inc. Fire Science & Engineering: Hughes Associates, Inc. Construction Manager: L.F. Driscoll Company. Maintenance Engineer: Entek Engineering. Exterior Wall: Heitmann & Associates, Inc. Air Quality/ Wind Tunnel: Rowan Williams Davies & Irwin, Inc. Vertical Transportation: Zipt Associates. Base Building Lighting Design: Thompson + Sears Lighting Design. Interior Lighting: The Lighting Practice. Acoustical: Shen Milsom & Wilke, Inc. Waterproofing/Roofing: Henshell & Buccellato.

The Langham Xintiandi & Andaz Shanghai Hotels
Shanghai, China
2011
Client: Shui On Properties Ltd. Design Principal: Joshua Chaiken. Managing Principal: Paul Katz. Senior Designer: Kazuki Katsuno. Project Manager: Richard Nugent. Job Captain: Edward Chang. Job Captain: Jae Hyun Chang. Job Captain: Bonnie Leung. Project Team: Shiju Balakrishnan, Peggy Chen, Rebecca Cheng, Sungwoo Heo, Arthur Hutchinson, Andreas Lange, Fanny Lee, Jing Liu, Beatriz Marin, Vien Nyugen, Carol Shi, Marcela Villarroel, Han Xu, Xiong Yi. Associate Architect: Leigh & Orange Design & Project Development. Government Liaison Architect: Architectural Design & Research Institute of Tong Ji University. Structural Engineer: AECOM Maunsell. M/E/P Engineer: Parsons Brinckerhoff (Asia) Limited. Curtain Wall: ALT Cladding & Design, Inc. Interior Design: Super Potato. Interior Design: Remedios Designers Inc. E & M Consultant: Squire Mech Shanghai Co., Ltd. Landscape Architect: Design Land Collaborative. LEED: Arup. Lighting Design: Isometrix. Lighting Design Consultant: Relux & Relux Lighting Design. Quality Surveyor: Davis Langdon & Seah.

The Ritz-Carlton, Toronto
Toronto, Canada
2009
Client: Graywood Developments Ltd. Managing Principal: Paul Katz. Managing Principal: A. Eugene Kohn. Senior Designer: Josh Chaiken. Project Manager: Gregory Waugh. Project Team: Luis E. Carmona, Peggy Chen, Chris Deckwitz, Gary Eversole, Sera Kimura, Christopher Knotz, Inkai Mu, Manon Pare, Nadine Pinkett, Poonam Sharma, Marcela Villarroel, Scott Wilson. Associate Architect: Page + Steele. Structural Engineer: Yolles Engineering. Mechanical Engineer: The Mitchell Partnership. Electrical Engineer: Hidi Rae Consulting Engineers. Life Safety & Code Consultant: Larden Muniak Consulting, Inc. Vertical Transportation: KJA Consultants Inc. Interior Design, Hotel: Hirsch Bedner Associates. Interior Design, Residential: Babey Moulton Jue & Booth. Landscape: Strybos & Associates. Traffic: BA Group. Soils: Terraprobe.

One Jackson Square
New York, USA
2010
Client: Hines. Design Principal: William Pedersen. Design Principal: Trent Tesch. Project Manager: Dominic Dunn. Project Team: Michael Kokora, Albert Lin, Lauren Schmidt. Associate Architect: Schuman Lichtenstein Claman Efron. Structural Engineer: Gilsanz Murray Steficek. M/E/P Engineer: WSP Flack & Kurtz. Geotechnical/Civil Engineer:

RA Consultants. Contractor: Hunter Roberts Construction Group. Sustainability: Steven Winter Associates. Acoustical: Cerami Associates. Vertical Transportation: Jenkins & Huntington. Historic Preservation: Higgins & Quasebarth.

21 Davies Street
London, United Kingdom
2004
Client: Capital & City PLC. Managing Principal: Lee Polisano. Senior Designer: Fred Pilbrow. Project Team: Cedra Ginsburg, Carl Gulland, Andrea Jung, Neil Merryweather, Alexander Steward, Ngozika Wamuo, Dean Weeden. Mechanical and Electrical Engineer: Grontmij (Roger Preston & Partners). Structural Engineer: Waterman Partnership. Construction Manager: Mace Limited. Landscape: Woodhams. Acoustical: Acoustic Design Ltd. Quality Surveyor: Mott Green Wall. Lighting: Lighting Design International Architectural Lighting. Land Surveyor: Michael Gallie & Partners.

Canal Walk
Incheon, Korea
2009
Client: Gale International and Posco E&C. Design Principal: Douglas Hocking. Managing Principal: Gregory Clement. Senior Designer: Eunsook Choi. Project Manager: Richard Nemeth. Project Team: Younhak Jeong, Jihyun Kim, Ji-Hwan Park, Amanda Paul, Emily Rhee, Ja-Young Yoon. Associate Architect: JINA Architects Co., Ltd. Structural and M/E/P Engineer: Arup.

First World Towers
Incheon, Korea
2009
Client: Gale International and Posco E&C. Design Principal: James von Klemperer. Managing Principal: A. Eugene Kohn. Managing Principal: Gregory Clement. Senior Designer: Brian Girard. Project Manager: Richard Nemeth. Job Captain: Russell Patterson. Project Team: Chihiro Aoyama, Alvaro Baile, Liana Bresler, Terri Cho, Thomas Coldefy, Ana Crittenden, David Goldschmidt, Knute Haglund, Lindsay Hance, Herman Ho, Rosanna Ho, Ricardo Ikeda, Kyu Hwan Jhin, Diarmuid Kelly, Seo Hyung Kim, Justin Kim, Jae Kwon, Kangsoo Lee, Soohee Lee, Leong-A Lee, Ming Leung, Tuan Luong, Jihwan Moon, Keon-soo Nam, Esther Park, Jinsuk Park, Meghna Patel, Temple Simpson, Anne Timerman, Daniel Treinen, Alan Salchow, Jose Sanchez, Christian Solano, Nancy Yin. Associate Architect: Kunwon Architects & Planners. Structural Engineer: Thornton Tomasetti. Structural Engineer: Weidlinger. M/E/P Engineer: Woowon Associates. M/E/P and FP Engineer: Cosentini. Contractor: Posco E&C. Landscape: Towers Golde.

Songdo Central Park
Incheon, Korea
2009
Client: Gale International and Posco E&C. Design Principal: James von Klemperer. Managing Principal: Gregory Clement. Senior Designer: Kevin Wegner. Project Manager: Thomas Holzmann. Project Team: Yanko Apostolov, Gregory Benjamin, Heather Bremensthuhl, Vincent Calabro, Eunsook Choi, Shih-I Chou, Luke Field, Jisop Han, George Hauner, Joon-hyuk Lee, Andrew McGee, Katherine Moya-Ramirez, Javier Oddo, Brian Ringley, Jason Rossitto, Morana Stipisic, Daniel Treinen, Thoas Tsang, Jed Weeks. Principal Consultant: Arup. Landscape: Ulysses Hedrick.

Songdo Convensia
Incheon, Korea
2008
Client: Gale International and Posco E&C. Design Principal: James von Klemperer. Senior Designer: Jisop Han. Project Manager: Richard Nemeth. Job Captain: Jorge Mendoza. Project Team: Brian Chung, Elie Gamburg, Markus Hocherl, Heejin Kim, Joon-Hyuk Lee, Chloe Li, Emily Menez, Nadine Pinkett, Daniel Treinen, Udoiwod Udoiwod. Architect of Record: Baum Architects. Structural and Mechanical Engineer: Arup. M/E/P Engineer: Hanil. Contractor: Posco E&C. Landscape Architect: Towers Golde.

Ilsan Cultural Center
Kyongki-Do, Korea
2007
Client: The Government of the City of Ilsan, Samoo Architects & Engineers. Design Principal: James von Klemperer. Senior Designer: Eunsook Choi. Project Team: Mark Foxworth, Esther Park, Laryssa Spolsky. Associate Architect: Space Group. Theater Consultants: Fisher Dachs. Acoustical: Jaffe Holden Acoustics, Inc.

U.S. Courthouse
Buffalo, USA
2011
Client: General Services Administration-Northeast and Caribbean Region. Design Principal: William Pedersen. Managing Principal: Robert L. Cioppa. Managing Principal: Jill N. Lerner. Senior Designer: Jerri Smith. Senior Designer: Trent Tesch. Project Manager: Laurie Butler. Job Captain: Devin Ratliff. Job Captain (Construction): Kevin Wegner. Project Team: Deborah Balters, Joseph Bausano, Theodore Carpinelli, Maria Conroy, Angela Davis, Pedro Calderon Donoso, Bruce Fisher, David Goldschmidt, Wendy Hanes, Ryan Hullinger, Merle Lange, Michael Marcolini, Florena Nemteanu, Kenichi Noguchi, David Ottavio, Russell Patterson,

Afshin Rafaat, Carlos Rodriquez, Rebecca Seamans, Sergy Yushchenko. Structural and Blast Engineer: Weidlinger Associates. M/E/P and FP Engineer: Arthur Metzler Associates. Civil Engineer: Watts Engineering. Contractor: Mascaro Construction Company. Curtain Wall: Gordon H. Smith Corporation. Exterior Maintenance: Entek Engineering. Geotechnical: Langan. Glass Veil Consultant: Dewhurst Macfarlane and Partners PC. Wind Engineering: Cermak Peterka Patersen, Inc. Code Consultants: Code Consultants PE. Sustainable Design/LEED: Natural Logic. Energy Analysis: Steven Winter Associates. Specifications: Heller & Metzer PC. Lighting: Thompson + Sears Lighting Design. Security: Kroll Schiff & Associates. Vertical Transportation: Persohn/Hahn Associates. Telecommunications: TM Technology Partners, Inc. Acoustical/Audio Visual: Polysonics, Inc. Cost Estimating: Vj Associates.

Dulles International Airport AeroTrain C-Gates Station
Chantilly, USA
2011
Client: Metropolitan Washington Airports Authority. Design Principal: William Pedersen. Managing Principal: Anthony Mosellie. Senior Designer: Kevin Cannon. Project Manager: Jennifer Taylor. Job Captain: Mark Townsend. Project Team: Lily Chiu, David Cunningham, Rachel Eck, Jackie Fung, Joshua Ginsburg, Liping Gong, Adolfo Guerrero, Kingsley Ho, Robert Jamieson, Calvin Lee, Jeremy Linzee, Mark Lyons, Vincent Poon, Charles Thomson, Basak Yuksel, Paulina Zamudi. Structural Engineer: Ammann & Whitney. Structural Engineer: Woods Peacock. M/E/P, FP: Arup. Civil Engineer: Alpha Engineering. Civil Engineer: Urban Engineers. Geotechnical: Schnabel Engineering. Civil Utility Structures: Burns Engineering. Civil Water Structures: A. Morton Thomas.

US Airways International Terminal One,
Philadelphia International Airport
Philadelphia, USA
2003
Client: US Airways. Design Principal: William Pedersen. Managing Principal: A. Eugene Kohn. Managing Principal: Anthony Mosellie. Senior Designer: Trent Tesch. Project Manager: Ayhan Ozan. Project Team: Alison Binks, Li-Min Ching, Michael Flath, Hidehisa Furuta, Bernardo Gogna, Zohed Jilal, Scott Loikits, George Murillo, Elaine Newman, Basak Yuksel. Associate Architect: Pierce Goodwin Alexander & Linville. Local Architect: Kelly/Maielle, Inc. Structural Engineer: Severud Associates. M/E/P Engineer: Robert C. Burns Associates. Mechanical Engineer: Mark Ulrick Engineers, Inc. Electrical Engineer:

Schiller & Hersh Associates, Inc. Civil/Geotechnical Engineer: Urban Engineers, Inc. Fire Protection: Code Consultants Incorporated. Airport Program Manager: DMJM Aviation. Airport Program Manager: Day & Zimmerman Infrastructure, Inc. Program and Construction Manager: Turner Construction Company. Specifications: Fred Petraglia Architectural Specification. Specifications: Donald Spector. Security: Glover Resnick & Associates. Passenger Flow Analysis/Simulation: JKH Mobility Services. Lighting Design: Domingo Gonzalez Design. Landscape: Synterra Ltd. Graphics/Interior Design: Daroff Design, Inc. Baggage Handling: BNP Associates, Inc. Audiovisual/Telecommunications: SITA. Acoustical & AV: Coffeen Fricke & Associates, Inc. Acoustics: Cerami Associates, Inc. Cost Management: Hanscomb Faithful & Gould., Inc. Hardware: Consulting Services Co. Hydrant/Fueling Systems: Roberts & Company. Vertical Transportation: John A. Van Deusen & Associates, Inc.

Roppongi Hills
Tokyo, Japan
2003
Client: Mori Building Company, Ltd. Design Principal: William Pedersen. Managing Principal: Paul Katz. Senior Designer (Office): Douglas Hocking. Senior Designer (Hotel): Joshua Chaiken. Senior Designer: David Malott. Project Team: Nicholas Chin, Dominic Dunn, Michael Flath, Steven Frankel, Johannes Knoops, John Lucas, Ko Makabe, Yayoi Ogo, Hisaya Sugiyama, Rashmi Vasavada, Mason White, Shinichiro Yorita. Engineering: Mori Building Co., LTD. Engineering: Irie Miyake Architects & Engineers. Structural Engineer: Arup. Contractor for Office: Obayashi & Kajima JV. Interior Architect: Jerde Partnership International, Inc. Hotel Interiors: Remedios Siembieda. Gallery Consultant: Jeffrey Deitch. Guggenheim Gallery Architect: Gluckman Mayner Architects. Landscape: EDAW.

Espirito Santo Plaza
Miami, USA
2004
Client: Estoril, Inc. Design Principal: William C. Louie. Managing Principal: A. Eugene Kohn. Senior Designer: Robert Whitlock. Project Manager: Peter Gross. Job Captain: Jorge Gomez. Job Captain: Charles Ippolito. Project Team: Michael Arad, Gertrudis Brens, Steve Carlin, Jae Hyun Chang, Christopher Ernst, Patrick Huang, Domenico Lio, John Lucas, Kavitha Mathew, Jeffery McKean, Jose Sanchez-Reyes, Daniel Treinen, Paul Yuen. Structural Engineer: Leslie Robertston Associates, RLLP. M/E/P Engineer: Flack & Kurtz Consulting Engineers. Civil Engineer: VSN Engineering. Coastal Engineering: Coastal Systems International, Inc. Coastal Engineering: EDC Corporation. Contractor: AMEC. Geotechnical: Langan. Curtain Wall: R.A. Heintges Architects. Exterior Building Maintenance: Citadel Consulting Incorporated. Code Consultant: Code Consultants Inc. Acoustics: Shen Milsom & Wilke, Inc. Landscape Architect: Architectural Alliance. Lighting Consultant: Tilotson Lighting. Traffic: David Plummer & Associates. Vertical Transportation: John A. Van Deusen & Associates, Inc.

One Central
Macau SAR
2009
Client: Hongkong Land Property Company. Managing Principal: Paul Katz. Senior Designer: Forth Bagley. Senior Designer: David Malott. Project Manager: Roger Robison. Job Captain: Nathan Wong. Project Team: Felix Burrichter, Yaminay Chaudri, Ju-Hui Chen, Patrick Clay, Keisuke Hei, Kingsley Ho, Sam Huang, Devin Koelbl, Alex Kong, Ping Kwan, Stephanie Lin, Jacqui Passando, Jakov Pinto, David

Tasman, Namita Tijoriwala, Nicholas Wallin, Zhe Wang, Steve Ybarra, Jiajun Yeo. Associate Architect: Wong & Tung International. Structural Engineer: Sin Yin Wai & Associates Ltd. Mechanical and Electrical Engineer: J. Roger Preston Limited. Contractor: Hip Hing Construction. Curtain Wall: Permasteelisa.

Palace 66
Shenyang, China
2010
Client: Hang Lung Properties Ltd. Design Principal: James von Klemperer. Managing Principal: Paul Katz. Senior Designer: Jeffrey Kenoff. Project Manager: Scott Springer. Project Manager: Gary Stluka. Project Manager: Bernard Chang. Job Captain: Audrey Choi. Job Captain: Alex Kong. Project Team: Camila Aldunate, Chantavudh Burusphat, Hanna Chang, Shang Chen, Thomas Coldefy, Kyu Hwan Jhin, Constantine Kalesis, Heejin Kim, Kangsoo Lee, Ming Leung, Saera Park, Sarah Schwartz, Sarah Smith, Donald Springer, Caroline Warlick, Scott Wilson. Architect of Record: P&T Architects & Engineers, Ltd. Associate Architect: China Northeastern Architectural Design and Research Institute. Structural Engineer: Arup. Mechanical and Electrical Engineer: J. Roger Preston Limited. Curtain Wall Consultant: Meinhardt (Hong Kong). Quality Surveyor/Cost Estimating: Davis Langdon & Seah. Landscape Architect: ADI Landscape Inc. Architectural Lighting: Brandston Partnership. Traffic: MVA Consultancy. Signage & Graphics: Graphia International Ltd.

China Central Place
Beijing, China
2007
Client: Beijing Guohua Real Estate. Design Principal: James von Klemperer. Managing Principal: A. Eugene Kohn. Senior Designer: Roger Klein. Project Manager: Richard Nemeth. Job Captain: Inkai Mu. Project Team: Darlington Brown, Eunsook Choi, Hughy Dharmayoga, Brian Domini, Liping Gong, Jisop Han, Keisuke Hiei, Manman Huang, Ming Leung, Jinseuk Lee, Alan Salchow, Jose Sanchez, Eric Smith, Udoiwod Udoiwod, Temple Simpson. Associate Architect (Office): East China Architectural Design & Research Institute Co. Ltd. Associate Architect (Residential): BIAD 1st Design Studio. Contractor: China Construction First Division Construction & Development Co. Exterior Wall Consultant: ALT Cladding & Design Inc. Fountain Design Consultant: CMS Collaborative. Landscape: EDAW. Lighting Design: Tilotson Lighting.

Northeast Asia Trade Tower
Incheon, Korea
2010
Client: Gale International and Posco E&C. Design Principal: James von Klemperer. Managing Principal: A. Eugene Kohn. Senior Designer: Jisop Han. Project Manager: Richard Nemeth. Job Captain: Jorge Mendoza. Project Team: Stephen Boehmke, Louis E. Carmona, Terri Cho, Brian Chung, Hughy Dharmayoga, Elie Gamburg, Emily Giese, Lisa Kenyon, Yoojung Kim, Joon-Hyuk Lee, Emily Menez, Brian Ringley, Daniel Treinen, Udoiwod Udoiwood, Chris White, Barrett Williams, Xiaolu Zhou. Associate Architect: Heerim Architects & Planners. Structural and M/E/P Engineer: Arup. General Contractor: Daewoo. Exterior Wall: ALT Cladding. Vertical Transportation and Façade Maintenance: Lerch Bates. Lighting: Tillotson Design Associates.

One Raffles Quay
Singapore
2011
Client: Keppel Land, Cheung Kong and Hongkong Land Joint Venture. Managing Principal: Paul Katz. Senior Designer: John Koga. Senior Designer: Kar-Hwa Ho. Project Manager: Richard Nugent. Job Captain: Inkai Mu. Project Team: Christopher Chan, Hogan Chun, Sebastian Cifuentes, Rena Gyftopoulos, Andreas Hausler, Jaskran Kalirai, Christopher Knotz, John Koga, Juan Lladser, Gaetane Michaux, Hisanori Mitsui, Jennifer Park, Marisa Yiu. Associate Architect: Architects 61. Mechanical, Electrical, Structural, Civil Engineer: Meinhardt (Singapore). Contractor: Obayashi Corporation. Curtain Wall Contractor: Benson Industries, LLC. Exterior Cladding: R.A. Heintges Architects. Landscape: Peridian Asia Pte, Ltd. Vertical Transportation (Concept Only): Van Deusen & Assocaites. Acoustics: Shen Milsom & Wilke. Traffic: Scott Wilson Pte, Ltd. Lighting: Isometrix Lighting & Design. Quality Surveyor: Davis Langdon & Seah. Signage & Graphics: Calori & Vanden-Eynden.

Marina Bay Financial Centre
Singapore
2011
Client: Cheung Kong (Holding) Limited, Hongkong Land Ltd., Keppel Land International Ltd. Design Principal: William C. Louie. Design Principal: Robert Whitlock. Managing Principal: Paul Katz. Senior Designer: Bruce Fisher. Senior Designer: David Goldschmidt. Project Manager: Thomas Holzmann. Project Manager: Ana Sortrel. Project Team: Shiju Balakrishnana, Heather Brumenthal, Felix Burrichter, Peggy Chen, Stephen Chen, Daniel Dadoyan, Pedro Calderon Donoso, Mark Gausepohl, Ryan Hullinger, Arthur Hutchinson, Gordana Jakimovska, Achyut Kantawala, Chris Knotz, Ming Leung, Jing Liu, Daniel Mannino, Maki Matsubayashi, Gustavo Ponzoa, Gary Tsai, Xiao Wang, Zhizhe Yu. Associate Architect: Aplusi Asia Pte Ltd. Associate Architect (Phase I): DCA Architect Pte Ltd. Associate Architect (Phase II): Architects 61. Structural and Civil Engineer: Meinhardt-MSCS. Mechanical and Electrical Engineer: Meinhardt-MSME. Main Contractor: Kajima-Tong Seng. Curtain Wall Consultant: ALT Cladding & Design, Inc. Curtain Wall Fabricator: Permasteelisa. Landscape: Tierra Design: Quantity Surveyor: DLS. Lighting: BPI.

New Songdo City
Incheon, Korea
2015
Client: Gale International and Posco E&C. Design Principal: James von Klemperer. Managing Principal: A. Eugene Kohn. Managing Principal: Gregory Clement. Senior Designer: Jinsop Han. Project Manager: Richard Nemeth. Project Team: Eunsook Choi, Anna Crittenden, Bruce Fisher, Pedro Font-Alba, Robert Goodwin, Chloe Li, Methanee Massirarat, Richard Nugent, Esther Park, Jennifer Park, Jose Sanchez, Hugh Trumbull, Kevin Wegner. Associate Architect: Kunwon Architects & Planners. Engineering: Arup.Landscape: Towers/Golde. Contractor: POSCO E&C.

Meixi Lake
Changsha, China
2010
Client: Gale International. Design Principal: James von Klemperer. Managing Principal: A. Eugene Kohn. Senior Designer: Trent Tesch. Project Manager: Richard Nemeth. Project Team: Yanko Apostolov, Flora Bao, Tiffany Broyles, Laurie Butler, Luis E. Carmona, Paulina Camus Carrion, Shih-I Chou, Brian Chung, Hughy Dharmayoga, Dara Goldberg, James Graham, Melanie Gutierrez, Chia-Chien Hsieh, Ting Huang, Gyu Jin Hwang, Justin Kim, Min Jin Kim, Min Young Kim, Rinor Komoni, Wells Landers, Hyunwoo Lee, Ting Li, Albert Lin, Kevin Lisoy, Jorge Mendoza, Donghwan Moon, Zhe Wang, Kevin Wegner, Christopher White, David Yang. Consultant: Arup.

Langfang International IDP
Langfang, China
2015
Client: Bestsun Energy Group. Design Principal: Douglas Hocking. Managing Principal: Inkai Mu. Senior Designer: Min Kim. Project Manager: Elaine Newman. Project Team: Gerardo Caliz, Bryon Frank, Jackie Fung, Stephen Lenz, Ryan Patterson, Jennifer Pehr, Charlie Portelli, Daniel Samton, Vivien Sin, Michael Young, Sung Yu.

BSD City Master Plan
Tangerang, Indonesia
2030
Client: Sinarmas. Design Principal: Robert Whitlock. Senior Designer: Bruce Fisher. Master Planner: Albert Wei. Master Planner: Jennifer Pehr. Job Captain: Rebecca Pasternack. Project Team: Diana Afonso, Brent Carson, Derek Chan, Ryan Consbruck, Nathan DeGraaf, Kristin Hawk, Allan Horton, Lisa Kenyon, Yu-Cheng Koh, Michael Linx, Daniel Mannino, August Miller, Michael Mitchell, Ben Van Nostrand, Hangul Park, Krista Raines, Sasha Rich, Natalya Shimanovskaya, Amanda Slaughter, Tom Tang, Atisha Varshney, Kevin Wegner. Infrastructure and Transportation Engineer: Arup.

Illustration Credits

Peter Aaron / ESTO, 9 (2), 154
Peter Aprahamian / Corbis, 115 (2)
Tom Arban, 73, 239
Btrenkel/istockphoto, 269 (5)
John Butlin, 184
John Chu / Kohn Pedersen Fox, 17 (1), 231, 257
Cityscape, 264
Crystal CG (Beijing), 356
Crystal CG (Shanghai), 352
DAAS, 303 (2)
Dbox, 303 (4), 364, 365
Michael Dersin, 195 (2)
Digital Mirage, 365
Driscoll, 222 right
H.G. Esch, 17 (2), 24, 36, 37, 63, 64, 65, 67, 68-69, 70, 71,
83, 84-85, 86, 87, 89, 91, 92-93, 95, 96, 97, 99, 100-101, 102,
103, 105, 106, 131, 132-133, 139, 145, 146-147, 164, 167,
168, 169, 175, 179, 181, 194 right, 195 (1 and 3), 196 right,
197, 198, 199, 200-201, 214 right, 216-217, 219, 220, 221,
249, 251, 262, 271, 272, 275, 308, 309, 310, 323, 324-325,
331, 329, 335, 348 top left
Elliot Fine, 9 (5)
Leonardo Finotti, 171, 172, 173
Fotosearch, 59
Tim Franco, 237
Wayne Fugi, 303
Gale International, 254-255, 348 bottom left
Shai Gil / Insite Photography, 73, 75
Dennis Gilbert, 11 (7), 13 (8)
Gregobagel / istockphoto, 115
Tim Griffith, 23 (2), 38, 44-45, 123-126, 128, 319, 328, 336-337
GUST, 273
Barry Halkin, 223
Harbour City, 180
Yum Seung Hoon, 281, 282-283
Hufton + Crow, 155 (3), 157, 158-159, 161, 203
Timothy Hursley, 269 (3, 6),
Hyatt Hotels, 236, 311
JaeSungE, 61, 62, 143 bottom, 253, 256, 259, 263, 276, 277,
278-279, 348 top right, 348 bottom right
Barbara Karant, 9 (3), 118, 119
Chang Kim, 305, 333, 365
Raimund Koch, 120-121, 155 (2), 163, 165, 204-205, 231 (4),
242-243, 244, 246, 364
Kunwon Architects, 260-261
Kawasumi Architectural Photography, 177
Mandarin Oriental, Macau, 321
Michael Moran, 206 right, 207, 208, 209, 210-211, 241, 245, 247
Mori Building Ltd., 19 (3), 33, 34-35, 40, 306-307, 365
Nacasa & Partners, 46-47
Shireen Nadir / AKA Communications, 74
Mike O'Dwyer, 196 left
David Ottavio / Kohn Pedersen Fox, 117

Youngchae Park, 140-141, 142, 143 top, 332
Park Hyatt Shanghai, 231 (2)
Justin Pipperger, 250
Jock Pottle / ESTO, 11 (6), 269 (1)
Paul Rivera / Archphoto, 115 (3)
Grischa Rueschendorf, 43, 48, 215, 320, 364
SCADIA, 269 (7)
David Seide, 269, 285, 286-287, 288, 289
Shikenchiku, 39, 41, 176
Kishin Shinoyama, 231 (1)
ShuHe, 234-235
Peter Sieger, 127,129
Tim Soar, 135, 136, 137, 160
Harold Sund / Getty Images, 57 (2)
Superview, 23 (2)
Tao Images Limited, 231 (3)
Eric Taylor, 291
Visualhouse, 360
Michael Weber / ESTO, 49
Whirler / istockphoto, 59 (3)
Alan Williams, 107
WilshireImages / istockphoto, 57 (1)
Don Wong, 269 (2)
Woodruff / Brown Photography, 212 right, 213, 224-225, 293,
294-295, 313, 314, 315, 316, 317
Fu Xing, 183, 185, 327
Zhang Guan Yuan, 90
Shen Zhonghai, 77, 78-79, 80, 81, 187

All other images provided by Kohn Pedersen Fox.

Acknowledgements

Producing this book required tremendous thought and careful consideration to reflect the growth and change of both KPF and the architecture profession since the firm's last monograph was published a decade ago. We would like to thank Jamie von Klemperer for his direction and critique over many months, as well as Paul Katz, Gene Kohn, Jill Lerner, Bill Louie, and Bill Pedersen for helping us shape the book into a refined and compelling anthology of 56 projects.

We would like to acknowledge the countless KPF staff around the world who helped with the compilation, revision and verification of the materials and data seen herein, including Julianna Haahs, Ting Huang, Jeanette Lin, Yoko Saigo, and Eunji Shim. Special thanks to Anastasia Laurenzi for her meticulous organization and attention to detail with editing and managing the plans and drawings.

Thank you to all of the photographers whose work is highlighted throughout the book, many of whom have been friends of KPF for decades. It is their talent that brings the essence of the firm's work to the public eye.

Many thanks to our friend Peter Murray for conducting such thoughtful and honest interviews over many hours in both New York and London, and for his input early in the process as the book took shape. Likewise, we would like to thank Ian Hawksworth, William Ko, Chris Ward, and Iris Weinshall for their time and contributions, and to Leslie Robertson whose interview unfortunately did not make it into these pages.

Lastly, we could not have completed the book without the support and assistance of the entire KPF marketing team, especially John Chu, whose knowledge of the firm and attention to detail was invaluable. We are also very grateful for the assistance and resources provided by Lowri Banfield, Susan Green, Susan Holbrook and Lena King.

Anita Franchetti and David Niles